A YEAR IN LA LA LAND

A YEAR
IN LA LA LAND

Wensley Clarkson

BLAKE

WENSLEY CLARKSON has fought off a soap star who tried to seduce his wife. He's battled over a megastar's clothes at a jumble sale. He's stopped his children from having sushi in their lunchboxes. He's confronted wild animals in his back garden. He's celebrated Thanksgiving with a transvestite. He's nearly lost a child on the edge of the Grand Canyon. He walked in on a game of chess... in a rundown doughnut store full of gang members. He was even at a dinner party when one Hollywood "player" sang the praises of telephone sex! He's ended up in the world's most famous strip joint with a Falklands hero. He's been to traffic school. He's endured a sensitive piece of surgery in the most celebrity studded hospital in the world. And he was nearly persuaded to invest in a nudist colony by a fading housewives' heart-throb.

Why? Because he made the momentous decision to swap the drab, grey streets of London for a long cherished dream to move his wife, four children plus cat and nanny to Hollywood. As a result, he also lived through mass flooding, earthquakes and the Los Angeles riots to uncover the secrets of survival in the most glamorous city in the world. Forget the over-priced hang-outs of the rich and famous, Clarkson instead takes us to the affordable restaurants, the incredibly good value motels and provides practical tips on the dos and don'ts of life in La La Land and the best places to visit in California.

He also reveals a fascinating insight into the day to day problems like housing, schooling, shopping and just plain old living in a society where out and out wealth provides the only social ladder to climb. *A Year In La La Land* is filled with anecdotes that will help every traveller to understand what makes this weird and wonderful city tick.

At a time when Hollywood has never been more popular – and never more reviled – Wensley Clarkson lifts the lid on La La Land with honesty and wit to offer tips and truisims all visitors to Los Angeles will appreciate.

A Year in La La Land takes us through the real ups and downs of life in California to provide unique revelations about what Tinsletown is really like when a perfectly normal family (sort of!) decides to make it their home.

WENSLEY CLARKSON, 36, was born and bred in London. As a journalist, he worked on the staff of the *Sunday Mirror* and *Mail On Sunday*. In 1987, he left newspapers to produce and direct television documentaries and commercials. Then in 1990, he wrote the highly acclaimed book *Dog Eat Dog* – a humourous account of life on the Fleet Street tabloids – which was followed by four best-selling true crime books. In 1991, he moved to Los Angeles with wife Clare and children Toby, Polly, Rosie and Fergus after being contracted by Twentieth Century Fox to write a screenplay based on one of his books. He has three other film projects in development at Hollywood studios and is currently working on a television movie starring Victoria Principal. He has also written more than two thousand freelance newspaper and magazine articles that have appeared in publications throughout the world.

Previously Published by Wensley Clarkson

Dog Eat Dog
Hell Hath No Fury
Like A Woman Scorned
Love You To Death, Darling
Doctors Of Death

I'm working on this book. I've written all the page numbers, now I've just got to fill in all the words.

Steve Wright

*Out of the condo
and into the car
means driving on freeways
when travelling far
rush hour makes gridlock
and speed is a crawl
the price of my living
in such urban sprawl
from Downtown LA
to Beverly Hills
life is a patchwork
of graffiti and frills
tourists take buses
to homes of the stars
someday I just might
take a rocket to Mars.*

LA My Way
by
Wanda Weiskopf

Published by Blake Publishing Ltd.
98-100 Great North Road, London N2 0NL, England

ISBN 1 85782 036 3

British Library Cataloguing-in-Publication Data:
A catalogue record for this book is available from
the British Library.

Typeset by BMD Graphics, Hemel Hempstead

Printed in Great Britain by BPCC Wheatons Ltd, Exeter

1 3 5 7 9 10 8 6 4 2

ACKNOWLEDGEMENTS

My thanks to John Blake. Also Mark Sandelson for his expert eye and Evzen Kolar for risking life and limb. And here's the rest: Rupert Maconick, John Bell, Barnaby Thompson, Graham Baker, Ant and Jeanie Bowman, Alex Wright, Deborah and Plinny Porter, Fiona De Rose, Deborah Kolar, Detective Fred Clapp, Michele Chapman, Pat King, Louise Frogley, John Glatt, Tewe Pannier, Peter Miller, Ginny Cerrella, Engelbert Humperdinck, Helena Springs, Nathalie Nompex, Peter Jayston, Suzanne and Godfrey Pye, Joe Paolella, Detective Mike Lee, Robert Lawrence, MC, David and Jenny Nichols, Roger Randall-Cutler, Barry Plumley, Sebastian Parker-Sed, Saverio Carubia, Nancy Smith, David Warner, Peter Wilson, Nathan and Hannah Crowley, Soung Lee, Jane West, Stephanie M, Una and Hugo Lind. Last, but by no means least, Clare, Toby, Polly, Rosie, Fergus and Bubbles.

DEDICATION

**TO MY MOTHER A MESSAGE: WHEN ARE YOU
COMING TO VISIT US IN LA LA LAND?**

CONTENTS

AUGUST

It's just another perfect day and I love LA.
Randy Newman

The early morning light bathed the bedroom in a gentle warmth. Through a gap in the curtains, I could see a humming bird hovering silently next to the window. It homed in on the orange head of a bird of paradise plant and took a brief breakfast before disappearing into the misty morning air. Outside, the swimming pool's filter system bubbled gently and I could hear a light plane's single engine in the distance.

I lay in bed and gazed up at the ceiling. No-one else was up and it seemed the perfect moment to reflect on things. We had just made the biggest decision of our lives and now there was absolutely no turning back. Moving my wife, four children, a nanny and a cat called Bubbles from the cosy, cluttered streets of Parson's Green, south west London, to the steaming hot, sprawling metropolis of Los Angeles would have been a fairly stressful operation just for a two week holiday. But when you transport the entire contents of seven people's lives on a permanent basis, it enters the realms of a military operation.

But we had somehow made it in one piece and now the biggest tests were to come...

"Daddy. You look dreadful."

Eleven-year-old Polly jumped on our bed with an almighty thump, snapping me out of my early morning catalepsy. She peered at my face with distaste. The previous night I had shaved off my moustache for the first time in fourteen years of married life. A drastic measure, but, as I explained to Clare, my wife, an essential one for a move to L.A. During an earlier trip to rent a house for our big move, I had found myself hemmed in the corner of a West Hollywood bar, in an area known as "Boy's Town", by three handsome, hunky looking, moustachioed fellows in skin tight jeans. A macho British friend explained why I was the centre of attention.

"It's that bog brush above your upper lip. It's like a badge in this town that says: 'Hi, I'm gay. Come fly with me.' You'll have to shave it off."

My first response was outrage. It's a free world isn't it? But then my friend took another approach.

"It'll make you look ten years younger and you won't have any of this nonsense to contend with..."

So there I was, on our first morning as residents in the City of Angels, suffering a barrage of abuse.

"She's right," my wife murmured, opening one eye. "You look awful. Your top lip looks as if it died a few years back. Grow it back."

I thought of my redneck, homophobic friend's advice, then of the inflight movie on the trans-Atlantic voyage the previous day, *Good Fellas* – full of moustachioed, macho Italians bedding every woman in sight – and I shrugged. If my family wanted me to grow back my moustache immediately, then so be it.

The entire household was up and demanding breakfast not long after dawn that first morning in La La Land – jet lag is not exactly conducive to heavy sleep. My tribe wanted food and who was I to argue? The odds in my family are always overwhelmingly against me. I'm just thankful that I have two boys and two girls. The thought of four daughters fills me with terror. Sex discrimination in large families is definitely to be encouraged.

2

So, we all piled into our rented Pontiac and headed off for a coffee shop that I had discovered during my earlier fact finding mission to Los Angeles. I just prayed that I could track it down easily...

Ten miles and one hour later, I finally located *Dukes Restaurant*, on Sunset Boulevard. It was fortunate that we took so long finding it. The entire family was so jet lagged we hadn't realised it was six-thirty in the morning and *Dukes* was only just opening its doors.

The waitress, a grandmotherly type with two front teeth missing, looked as if she had just walked off the set of *Badlands*.

A sign behind her head read: "Every morning I get up and make instant coffee and I drink it so I have the energy to make the real thing."

Dukes is a popular hangout with rock n'roll industry types. The Boss and Madonna can often be found sitting in opposite corners of the coffee shop, studiously ignoring each other's presence of course. But the waitress was more than delighted to get a "real family" in there for a change. She smiled warmly as we scanned the menus.

I chose *Dukes* to be our first port of call as La La Land residents because I had been told that this long-established coffee shop served one of the finest breakfasts in town. And in health conscious Los Angeles there aren't too many of these places left. In the classic coffee shop, motherly waitresses call everyone "Honey" and cases filled with delicious looking pies are lined behind the counter. Traditional American breakfasts are an art form in themselves; you only know you've had the real thing if you feel like you've put on half a stone in half-an-hour.

Within seconds of arriving our waitress was filling our cups with coffee and awaiting our orders and a few minutes later we were tucking into vast plates of bacon and pancakes, swimming in the obligatory maple syrup.

My tribe of four insisted on also ordering hot chocolate, in *Dukes* a meal in itself with enough calories in each cup to ruin any starlet's career.

"Can we come here every day for breakfast daddy?"

"Please Daddy. Please!!!"

I looked up at the hundreds of autographed photos of everyone from James Dean to Marlon Brando that line one wall of the coffee shop and began to suspect that my time might come much sooner than expected if I agreed to pig out at *Dukes* every morning.

When the bill came I realised why so many LA residents eat out most days of their lives. It was just $36 for seven of us.

Sunset Boulevard was starting to come to life as we walked out into the hot, humid August air. It was seven thirty in the morning, but we were still on London time. I looked up at one of the vast billboards that line a one-mile stretch of this famous street. A thirty foot high cut-out of Arnold Schwarzenegger looked down at us announcing *Terminator Two – Judgement Day*. Uzi tucked under his right arm. Muscles rippling. There was no way Arnie could manage a gut-bashing breakfast in *Dukes* every day – those firm biceps would turn to flab in weeks. He was probably enjoying a little yoghurt and muesli at that very moment. If only he realised what he was missing!

We ventured down to Venice Beach soon after arriving in Los Angeles because we'd been told it's one of the places you have to see. The nearest thing to it back in Britain is the Portobello Road, in west London, on a Saturday afternoon. But Venice is street theatre with a difference.

His stage was the sidewalk beside the beach, cluttered with chains, broken glass and a bed of nails. He was pacing like a caged animal, his jeans sagging from his grey, wirey torso, his black rimmed eyes squinting at the crowd of

4

tourists encircling him. This was just a perfectly normal Sunday afternoon scene in the wackiest town in La La Land.

Clare and I and the children watched on tiptoe as the showman planted his feet wide apart and tucked a railroad spike into one nostril before hammering the iron stake right up his nose. Moans and shrieks rose from the crowd of onlookers. A few squeamish people covered their eyes, while others cast furtive looks at their companions. Toby, Polly, Rosie and Fergus just laughed as the Human Blockhead tried to nail his nose to the back of his head. Perhaps my kids are a bit too worldly for their own good.

Apparently, the Human Freak Show – that part of Americana which dominated fair grounds until half way through this century – has made a monster of a comeback at places like Venice. The thousands of people who pour onto the Venice boardwalk each weekend have provided this bizarre collection of sideshows with a perfect income.

Other attractions include the "Amazing Mr Lifto" who dangles two steam irons and a cinder block from the rings in his pierced nipples. Or there is Dolly the Doll Lady, an aging circus dwarf who feeds live slugs to a sword swallower – as they both dance along to a *Talking Heads* soundtrack on the scratchy stereo.

Another crowd pleaser is Matt "The Tube" Crowley, a former Montana pharmacist who specialises in swallowing several quarts of beer, chocolate sauce and ketchup through a tube in his nose. His encore is to pump the bile beer up again.

The children were transfixed and made me donate generous tips at the end of each eccentric performance, arguing that it was less ghoulish than the guts and thunder megadeaths committed on television and in the movies.

We knew a number of people in Tinseltown before we decided to move lock, stock and barrel across the Atlantic. Admittedly most were British – but then there are more than

250,000 Brits in California.

You can divide the Brits here into three categories:

1 The ones who've never changed and you know you'd just as easily be friends with in LA or London.

2 The ones who become corporate-minded, serious-thinking (and ultimately boring) mini-movie moguls, despite being good fun when they lived in England.

3 The ones you'd never want to know in England anyway, so why change the habit of a lifetime and make friends with them just because you're both living in the same country?

I mention all this because we were asked to a dinner party in the Hollywood Hills by some old friends from England who'd moved out a year earlier.

I had imagined weeks, if not months of living in a social desert where there were few dinner invites and an empty calendar. So, with the kids safely tucked up in bed and the nanny in charge just like she had been in London, we eagerly set off for dinner in the Hollywood Hills.

There are certain conclusions to be drawn about people who choose to live in the steep hills overlooking the rabid, happy dog of a city that goes by the name of Los Angeles. If caution is not a way of life to everyone who has to face the twists, turns and runaway descents of these neighbourhoods, then it must be because they were born lucky.

We were navigating a terrifying mountain road up into the Hollywood Hills. Clare – who's afraid of heights – squinted at the glittering lights spread below us like some vast pinball machine, while I struggled to read my essential *Thomas Guide* (the equivalent to the *London A-Z*).

Suddenly, the Pontiac hit a huge pothole and lurched towards the edge of what appeared to be a vertical drop. Trying to read the mapbook at the same time as driving is an ill-advised habit.

Luckily, the Pontiac's power breaks were effective.

Another two feet and we might have been catapulted into an involuntary lover's leap, ending in the roof of someone's house more than a thousand feet below. This is a city where people regularly land their private airplanes on motorways. But flying cars...

We recovered our composure and finally made it to the top of Laurel Canyon – a vast hilly area that collars the city. We had just travelled sixteen miles, including a hill that seemed higher than Mount Snowdon, and this was considered the equivalent of popping around the corner to a friend's for dinner.

Three fit-looking characters in red jackets approached as I slowed down to check the street numbers. I looked nervously at Clare as they began surrounding the car. These guys seemed too well dressed to be robbers, but maybe they were an upmarket gang of hoods from south central LA prowling the Hollywood Hills in tuxedos looking for wealthy victims.

"Just leave the keys in the car please sir."

I couldn't believe it. Our host and hostess – who only a year earlier had lived in a rather tatty 1930s three-bed semi south of the Thames – had hired valets to park their dinner guests' cars. Valets at a restaurant I understood, but at a dinner party for ten people?

Rough and tumble dinner parties where everyone mucks in don't tend to exist in certain homes in Los Angeles. In their place are designer events where the wife – who presumably cannot cook – hires staff to prepare a delicious spread, via the West LA edition of the *Yellow Pages*. And like our hostess, they rarely admit where they find their "super chef" for fear that others might hire the chef for a rival dinner party.

Faced with the possibility of another 5am alarm call from our jet-lagged kids the next morning, we decided not to stay late at our first Hollywood dinner party and after a less-than-sparkling evening set off down the twisting, winding roads of Laurel Canyon. But our night was far from over.

Turning into Sunset Boulevard to head west towards our home in Brentwood, I spotted the name of the main road that ran just near the house. I didn't realise this particular street was a least 20 miles long.

"Let's take a quicker route," I said confidently, pleased to have spotted a short cut home.

Ten miles later, I was feeling less confident. The safe suburban streets of west LA had been replaced by derelict car parks and rundown apartment blocks. None of the surrounding area looked familiar.

"Why don't you stop and ask someone the way?"

Clare's request may have seemed reasonable but it was gradually dawning on me that it was ten past midnight on a Saturday night and we had just entered central Los Angeles, where the average monthly murder rate is around sixty.

Gangs of people were roaming the dimly lit streets. Flashing blue and green neon lights from overhead buildings illuminated alleyways where huddles of homeless were sleeping. We had entered no-man's land, the part of the city everyone talks about, but avoids after nightfall.

Suddenly, I heard a police siren in the distance. I prayed it would come my way so that at least I'd have the long arm of the law nearby for protection. But the siren faded and instead I heard the distinctive throb of a burned out V-8 engine as a low-slung two door Chevy rolled up alongside us. Six faces peered in our direction.

LA Times headlines were rushing through my mind. "British Couple Mugged and Killed," was the recurring theme. How could I have been so stupid? We had managed to get lost in a war zone after just one day in the City of Angels.

"You've got to stop and ask someone."

A bus pulled up alongside us at some traffic lights. I was

about to ask the driver for directions, but then I remembered the newspaper story I'd read the previous day revealing that at least 50% of the city's bus drivers were registered crack addicts.

And then I spotted a policeman standing on the corner of a deserted junction. As I slowed down, his eyes darted towards me, but as I struggled to wind down my window he made no attempt to approach me. Instead, he began to take out his gun. I didn't know what to do. I could either step my foot on the accelerator and try to escape before he blasted at me or I could continue my request for assistance and ignore the fact a .38 Special was about to be pointed at me.

I was later to discover that virtually all officers also carry a back-up gun strapped to their leg, a pump action shotgun in their cruisers and an electronic tazer to still the deadly frenzy of PCP spasms with a 50,000-volt jolt. One cop I know told me that hardened criminals train themselves in prisons on how to take out a policeman's gun.

"They'll talk to you and try to inch closer. A lot of new officers won't think about it, but as soon as someone gets close to me I say, 'Step over there!' My gun leg will always be back so they're going to have to reach across."

He also said rather ominously: "Violence is a way of life here. We know guns are out there. We know they're in every house and if you walk up to a door here they're likely to kick your ass. If they see you positioning the car the wrong way they'll jump on you. There are really no second chances in this city."

"I am so sorry to trouble you. Do you know the way to Brentwood?"

Back in La La Land that night, I put on my finest English accent. Many years earlier, I had learnt that a good English voice relaxes most Americans the moment they hear it. The cop put his gun back in his holster, visibly relieved.

Maybe if I had said something like: "Hey man, how do I get to downtown...?" I might have been filled with lead before I even mentioned Brentwood.

"Brentwood? You're kidding me?"

My request was obviously a bit like asking a policeman in Potter's Bar the way to Chelsea.

"How in hell's name did you get here? This is a dangerous area at this time of night. You shouldn't even be here."

A carload of youths slowly passed by and I noticed the officer's hand return to his gun. His fingers gripped the handle as he watched the car cruising by. Then he relaxed once more and gave us clear, concise instructions on how to get out of one of the most deadly districts in the world.

Many uniform cops moonlight as security guards in department stores, office blocks and even private homes. It must seem like easy money after a night out on patrol on these streets.

As I drove off, the radio on his Kawasaki parked nearby crackled into action: "Shooting on Third and Main. Please respond..."

A few weeks later I saw a piece in the *LA Times* headlined, "August – the Hottest, Bloodiest Month" which revealed that August is the most life-threatening month in the La La Land calendar.

In laid-back fashion, the article's first paragraph stated: "It's August again, that time of year that compels some folks to leave their stuffy homes, seek relief from the summer heat and commit murder."

Since 1988, there has been an average of 88 killings each August which, said the *Times*, "police attribute in part to frayed tempers brought on by the heat."

LA police officer Cruz Lopez told the paper casually: "It's nothing out of the ordinary; it's just considered a bad weekend."

The weekend he was talking about just happened to be

when I managed to get lost in the most violent city centre in the world.

Consider this. In a recent study of handgun deaths it was revealed that 8 died in Britain, 24 in Switzerland, 18 in Sweden, 77 in Japan, 23 in Israel, 4 in Australia... and almost 12,000 in the United States.

There are more than 20,000 murders every year in the USA. In plain terms, anyone here has a one in 12,000 chance of being bumped off each year. But, having said all that, most of these killings occur in highly populated, poor neighbourhoods or amongst criminal circles.

After visiting the States more than thirty times in the past fifteen years, I have devised my own special set of rules and regulations for avoiding problems in potentially dangerous areas of La La Land.

And here they are, my dirty dozen precautions that might just help you avoid meeting the city's angels before your time:

1 Never look as if you're lost. Try to retain an air of confidence, even if you don't happen to know where the hell you are! The moment you let those defences drop, you'll become an easy target for all sorts of weirdos.

2 If you find yourself wandering through a rough neighbourhood, hail a taxi and *get outta* there. It's relatively simple to work out if the area is risky. Count the number of people on the sidewalks. The more there are, the more dangerous it is.

3 If someone approaches you for money in a threatening manner, don't look him or her in the eyes; just keep on walking. If you make eye contact, he'll simply be encouraged. Admittedly, there are many pan handlers who are simply interested in the cost of a beer and nothing more. But some want the contents of your wallet and once you've taken

it out of that snug pocket, it could end up costing you your life.

4 Never lose sight of your handbag or briefcase. Even in a restaurant keep it nearby at all times. A friend once had his case lifted from under a table by an umbrella handle!

5 Don't carry any more cash on you than you really need. La La Land is a credit crazy society. If people think you have lots of green notes, they'll start taking an unhealthy interest in you.

6 Don't leave valuables in your car. Even the trunk can be unsafe in certain areas. La La Land residents frequently put signs in their car windows saying: "Don't bother breaking window. Radio already stolen." Which says it all.

7 Never wear expensive jewellery on the streets. It encourages the muggers, pan handlers, weirdos and just about every other undesirable.

8 At the airport, watch your luggage like a hawk. Dozens of cases disappear every day from LA's main international airport.

9 Park your car as near as possible to any restaurant or house you are visiting. It is often worth the $3 to $5 it costs for a valet in exchange for a safe, short walk.

10 Don't stare at people in cars next to you at traffic lights. At best, they'll probably try and burn you off from the lights. At worse, they'll take a liking to your automobile and decide to follow you home to rob you.

11 If you're British and in trouble, ham up that accent for all it's worth – it might just help! I once encountered six shady looking characters outside a supermarket on Sunset Boulevard just as I was about to get into my car. The conversation went something like this:

Mugger 1: "Yo man. Where ya headin'?"

Yours truly: "I'm looking for the police station."

Mugger 2: "What d'you say? Where you from?"

Mugger 3: "You talk real strange."

Yours truly: "Would any of you gentlemen know where the police station is?"

Mugger 1: (a truly incredulous look on his face): "Police station? Down the road, second on the right."

At this point, his friends looked completely confused and gave up any thoughts of assault with a deadly weapon and simply wished me a speedy journey.

Mugger 2: "You take care man. It's dangerous out there."

I subtly switched on the internal door locking system the moment I got in my car and managed to beat a hasty retreat.

And finally,

12 If you do end up being mugged, just take it like a man (or woman) and don't fight back. Give him or her the money and count your lucky stars nothing worse happened!

Obviously, I cannot guarantee that my dirty dozen rules will ensure your safety on the streets of La La Land, but so far (touch wood) they've worked for me.

You cannot exist in Los Angeles without a car – it's as simple as that. There are more than 200 cities in the metropolitan area of Los Angeles. The population of thirteen million uses 1500 miles of freeways and an incredible 12,500 miles of other surface roads. Not surprisingly, there are nearly five and a half million registered vehicles. And at $300 a week for a rented vehicle, I was feeling intense financial pressure to own one of them myself.

A seasoned La La Land expatriate was adamant about the type of car we should purchase.

"Those early seventies convertibles are brilliant," he assured me, conveniently forgetting that I have a family of six. I had other ideas, however. I wanted the biggest, least fashionable car I could find, for as little money as possible.

Getting a car on HP was an impossibility. We would not be considered credit worthy by America's loan corporations until we had set up bank accounts and obtained VISA cards in triplicate. (This is a country where mortgage defaulters lose their homes after missing out on one monthly payment. A line of credit is your key to happiness here).

So, armed with a king's ransom of $2,000, I bought a *Car Trader* magazine (equivalent of the *Exchange and Mart*) and began scouring the pages for a suitable heap of junk. The magazine features photographs of every vehicle. There were numerous contenders, but the perfect 'boat' turned out to be a metallic peat 1982 Chevrolet Caprice Station Wagon that made my old Volvo estate back in Britain look like a Mini Clubman.

It was the beginning of a love affair with a car that most people in this town consider an eyesore. I love every vulgar thing about my Chevy, from the tacky brown upholstery to the ridiculous Jaguar-style spoked hubcaps. My *boat* has the two luxurious requirements essential in Los Angeles. Cloth seats and fully operational air conditioning. It gets hot and sticky in those traffic jams.

One friend proudly splashed out quite a few thousand dollars more on a flashy second-hand BMW with plastic seats and broken down a.c. He has regretted the day he bought that car ever since.

Other friends were appalled at my purchase.

"How could you drive around in an American car? They're so badly made."

I've been lectured many times by La La Landers on why their country's car manufacturers are dead and buried. All self-respecting Americans in tinseltown buy German or Japanese.

Japanese cars are quite a social symbol. In fact, the Honda Accord is the best selling car in the state and people talk about their flimsy Nipponese pieces of metal on wheels as if they were works of art. As for the Germans, there are more Mercedes, Porsches and BMWs in California than in the Fatherland!

But I feel safer and more secure in my oversized Chevy than in any more luxurious model. In recent years, there has been a steep rise in so-called "drive-home" robbery in LA. Basically, it goes something like this. Two criminals out for a drive spot a single person motoring past them in a flashy Merc, Porsche or Honda and decide to follow him home. As the unsuspecting motorist parks outside his house, the two villains jump out, point a gun in the victim's ribs, demand all his jewellery/cash and then steal his car.

Every cop I've met during various writing assignments here has told me that these villains are not interested in most American cars, and certainly not ten-year-old Chevy Caprices overbrimming with children and popcorn.

The other great thing about driving a slightly battered old car is that everyone gets out of your way. Motorists in their gleaming new (debt riddled) cars live in fear of being hit by the tens of thousands of uninsured drivers in battered autos. I happen to be fully covered, but I do feel amused every time a fragile Japanese sportscar swerves out of my way on the freeway.

This is also a city where gangs of scam artists spend each day cruising the freeways trying to engineer car crashes, in order to make outrageous insurance claims.

Only recently, one such artist was charged with murder after he pulled in front of a truck on a freeway and caused an accident that cost one of the passengers his life. When the police raided the scam artist's home they found "scripts", written like Hollywood screenplays, which he used to rehearse exactly what should be said after any accident to ensure a maximum payout. This man is the first person in the U.S. ever to be tried on a murder charge as a result of what the *LA Times* described as a "purported automobile insurance scam." The end result of all this, of course, is high car insurance rates.

Our first month in La La Land could have been a horrendously expensive process, but we managed to cut our moving costs considerably by purchasing second-hand furniture.

Most people in Los Angeles want new houses, new furniture and new cars. For a slightly sloppy family from London, this can spell a thousand opportunities to set up home very cheaply. We had only shipped the bare essentials over from Britain, so within days of arriving, we infiltrated the deeply frowned upon world of the garage sale.

Garage sales are the equivalent of jumble sales in Britain, but with one big difference: you don't need to be raising money for charity or a new church roof. In the good old U S of A, you can spend your weekends setting up a pile of junk on your front lawn and selling it for your own profit.

For some La La Landers, the thought of buying used knives and forks or glasses fills them with horror; you might be risking AIDS, the plague, even maybe the dreaded flu that every inhabitant of this city tends to suffer from at least five times a year. Ironically, the well-heeled areas of Brentwood, Beverly Hills and Bel Air are considered the prime garage sale areas in the city. This causes deep resentment amongst millionaire residents. The *LA Times* reported how Beverly Hills city officials had imposed a $25 fee for garage sale permits to try and discourage them. A City Councilman told the paper: "A guy's got an $800,000 home and he has to look at a bunch of garbage on his neighbour's lawn." I suppose that's one way of putting it.

The poorer residents from the centre of the city go out for a drive on a Saturday or Sunday looking for bargains in the affluent West Side. Many car crashes are caused at weekends by pick-up trucks filled with vast families suddenly stopping on busy residential streets because they've spotted some second-hand marguerita mix machine in amongst the junk of a garage sale.

But picking up the Chevy for such a snip had given me

a taste for a bargain. We spotted a Chesterfield look-alike for $10 and desk for $20 on a tatty sidewalk, and over the following few weeks managed to furnish our entire house from garage sales. If we admitted to some La La Landers where we got our furniture, they'd probably refuse to sit down on the sofa for fear of catching something nasty.

American furniture is very well built, and although much of it might look ghastly if plonked in the middle of the Queen's drawing room, it doesn't look so bad in our single storey dwelling (bungalow to the rest of us) in Brentwood, Los Angeles.

Forget the language. Forget the close ties that are supposed to exist between our two nations. America is and always will be a foreign land. But one of the incredible things about Los Angeles is that about 75% of all its residents are 'transients', just like the rest of us. According to the 1990 U.S. census, California is still experiencing huge population growth, including a 62% surge in the number of Latino residents. But the biggest population explosion is amongst the Asians – a whopping 119% over the past ten years.

This vast blend of cultures can bond people closer together. Take my local newsagent in Brentwood. A few days after arriving in La La Land, I went in search of a good friendly newspaper shop where I could get the masses of magazines and papers that are my staple diet.

"You get 'em outta machines on the sidewalk here buddy," said one American friend, referring to the newspaper machines that have become part of American tradition. But he was wrong.

In most areas of Los Angeles there are privately owned newsstands. They look a bit like larger versions of those little sheds covered in a sea of newsprint that still exist in places like The Aldwych and Paddington Station, back in London town.

I was delighted when I came across such an establishment just half a mile from our home in the green leafy suburbs run by a Mr B. Patel.

I haven't asked him what the 'B' stands for, but then I never asked my newsagent back in Parson's Green either, and his name was Patel as well!

I was sorely tempted to ask if he was related to my newsagent back in London. But I resisted the temptation. I had a newsagent called Patel. What more could I possibly want from life?

In those first tentative weeks of living in La La Land, the fact that my local newsagent was named Patel made me feel more at home than anything else.

The landlady of our new home – a rather ill-humoured Iranian woman – had warned me never to open a strange-looking trap door on the floor of the garage of our new home. So within days of arriving in LA, my kids were nagging the life out of me to do just that.

All I knew was that beneath the one-inch thick metal door was a nuclear fallout shelter, which had been built along with the house, at the time of Kennedy's Cuban Missile crisis in 1962. In those days, escape from the holocaust of nuclear war was uppermost in most LA residents' minds and a number of sharp entrepreneurial builders had made fortunes out of constructing cramped little shelters six feet beneath the gardens of many houses.

Thirty years later, on a steaming hot August night, I came to realise how reassuring these paranoid contraptions are to your average LA resident. Less than three weeks after our arrival in the United States, a group of gung-ho generals tried to halt the decline of communism in the Soviet Union – while many of the residents of Brentwood held their breath and waited for the outbreak of World War Three.

In our quiet, tree-lined street, the neighbours were

already nervously calculating whether there was enough space in the fallout shelters in the area for them all.

"You should re-stock the shelter with food," the elderly woman opposite told Clare.

The whole street was taking the threat of a Russian nuclear attack very seriously. Of course, we were being typically British about it.

"But you don't seriously..."

Within another hour, two other residents had called to inquire about our fallout shelter. War was on the horizon and they seemed to be suggesting we should invite them to spend Armageddon with us in our underground room.

Soon we got swept up by the H-Bomb fever and mounted operation clear-out-nuclear-shelter. And so it was I found myself reluctantly staring down into the dark and dingy room six feet below the floor of the garage.

"I'm not going down there. It could be full of rats," I whispered.

I was the fearless father who'd recently paid his son $5 to remove a rat that was floating on the surface of our pool. No way was I going down into that fallout shelter.

Eventually, Clare ventured down with all four kids in hot pursuit. Apart from some antique tins of baked beans and a pungent damp aroma, the shelter wasn't much to write home about. Three hours later the Russian revolution caved in, Boris Yeltsin became a household name and we padlocked that trap door, hopefully, for ever.

SEPTEMBER

LA is where things happen. Lotsa action.
Limitless accessibility. Love arousal.
Ev Morris

When Southern Man by Neil Young came on the car radio I knew we had really arrived in La La Land. I hadn't heard it for at least ten years, yet every word came flooding back as I sang along.

In the two back rows of seats in the Chevy, my kids cringed. Alongside me, Clare looked pained. They obviously did not understand. This was one of the great classic songs of the early seventies. I was soon flashing back to muddy pop festivals and pleasant smelling cigarettes.

"Daddy. Please! It's so embarrassing."

Polly was official spokesperson for her three brothers and sisters. They were all most concerned that Mr and Mrs Average in the Ford compact alongside us in a traffic jam would be shocked and horrified by my serenade to hippy-dom, but not in the least bit worried that we were stuck in a two mile line of vehicles that just happened to stretch across the Golden Gate Bridge in San Francisco (which is painted red, by the way, despite its name).

Before leaving Parsons Green, we promised we would get out and about the moment we hit California and here we were on our first big trip.

We had just completed a drive that was the equivalent of going from London to Newcastle and back in a day. San Francisco maybe a small hop to the locals, but don't forget the entire state is more than twice the length of Britain.

We had been told to take the faster freeway route north

21

to Tony Bennett's favourite city, and return to Los Angeles on the Pacific Coast Highway, so that the car would be on the ocean side for the stunning views.

Neil Young and I were reaching our crescendo, completely ignoring the protests that were being hurled at me from all directions, when about one third of the way across the Golden Gate the traffic began to slow down. A bank of fog hung in the air a few hundred yards ahead, a sheer wall of white. As the Chevy hit the fog, the sound of the engines of the cars became more muffled and we nervously crawled along the smooth blacktop. But the fog lifted as we reached the other side and the sun and blue skies were clear above San Francisco. We had arrived.

We stayed at the Sheraton Hotel in the centre of the city, which is well located for all the classic tourist activities, but expensive and we might as well have stayed in a $15-a-night motel because we only used our rooms to sleep in. The rest of the time was spent exploring the streets and sights of this remarkable city.

San Francisco residents tend to look down their noses at La La Landers and *vice versa*. San Francisco has the gentle, cluttered, clapboard feel of a coastal city where people take their time doing anything, whereas LA is a sprawling mass of rapidly constructed housing where everything has to be done yesterday. People live in these two cities for entirely different reasons and that's probably the way it will always be.

One of the things about having such a big family is that you have to organise everything very doggedly. The result is that we are always the first ones at any kid's party, airport or railway station. We are also always the first ones up every morning, which was a great advantage waiting for a tram to the famous Fishermen's Wharf area of San Francisco. You need to get there early to avoid the horrendous queues at the tram stops.

From Fishermen's Wharf you can take a vast assortment of boat trips out into the bay. We took a trip to Alcatraz Jail – permanent island home to some of America's most notorious villains until its closure thirty years ago. A slight mist drifted across the tiny island as we stepped ashore, along with about fifty other touristos snapping furiously away with their sureshots. Being huddled together like pigs in a pen as we were shown around the once fearsome prison somehow ruined the creepy atmosphere, which the kids had been relishing. But maybe without any angry, bitter faces staring out from behind the iron bars, it wouldn't have been the same anyway.

Back on the mainland we took a trip into Chinatown early that evening. Here, stalls line the pavements, selling a vast range of delicacies from fortune cookies to crispy pancake rolls. The atmosphere is electric – brightly coloured banners over every store, the streets buzzing with crowds of every race, religion and colour. The narrow sidewalks of San Francisco with their two and three-storey buildings make it feel more like Europe than the United States.

I had always wanted to bounce a car down the bumpy and frighteningly steep hills of San Francisco ever since seeing Karl Malden and Michael Douglas do it in that popular 70s cop series *The Streets of San Francisco*. The great thing about having bought a cheap, tough car is that you don't really care about a few bumps and scrapes, and the vastness of the Chevy makes you feel immune from danger.

After consulting our map for the steepest gradient and climbing it slowly, as if it were a roller coaster, we hit Union Street. The children were tense with excitement and Clare was in near hysterics because of her fear of heights, but fingers crossed, I assured them all that this was going to be fun.

At the top of the hill, I held the boat steady for a few

moments to build up the tension and then we began the descent.

The first hump of the hill we hit at a modest 20 miles per hour. The car lifted momentarily but it was nothing more than a very brief stomach flyer. But we reached the next lip at a much higher speed and the boat literally took off for a few feet. There was no stopping us now. We bumped and grinded our way down that hill at such a severe angle that I feared the Chevy would simply slip out of control. Five minutes and at least a dozen humps later, we came to the bottom of the hill and my carload of excited kids screamed for more. What could I do? I swung the boat around and headed back up. For two hours we flew up and down that hill. The children said afterwards that those car rides were one of the most memorable things about our trip to San Francisco.

In comparison the tram appeared a charmingly anti-quated form of transport. But it's also a precarious way to travel around the busy streets of a bustling city. If you've got young children, be warned! We almost lost our four-year-old on numerous occasions as he leaned too far out over the edge of the crowded tram. The risk of decapitation is high!

The 400-miles plus drive home on the twisting, turning Pacific Coast Highway was the highlight of the trip; miles of deep, blue ocean, pelicans skimming the surface, hawks hovering over hilltops, lush pasture rolling like velvet under the sea mist. This route takes nearly twice as long as Interstate Five, but it's worth every single extra minute of travel time.

We left San Francisco just before dawn to take advantage of the brilliant early morning light, stopping for breakfast at a hippy-run coffee shop perched ominously on the edge of a 500 foot cliff and then it was on to the seaside community of Carmel.

Clint Eastwood, who used to be mayor of this tidy little

principality, was disappointingly nowhere in sight as we hit Carmel's immaculate streets. But he still owns a restaurant in the area where you can buy "Dirty Harry Burgers", of course. Carmel actually resembles a film set more than a real town because it's so perfect, not even a blade of grass out of place. And Carmel is very expensive.

We drifted from hotel to hotel in the Chevy, trying to find a couple of affordable rooms. Finally, we found the Carmel River Inn, a quaint little place on the edge of town that consisted of a group of two-bedroom log cabins. At $45 a night for accommodation it was a snip, and it was much more fun than staying in a chain motel.

That evening we ventured into the centre of Carmel. Scores of people were on the streets and the atmosphere was more like a village on a Greek island, rather than sophisticated California. Apparently 100,000 cars cruise through this tiny town (population 4,800) on a busy summer weekend. There are more than 50 restaurants but thankfully McDonald's and Kentucky Fried Chicken have been banned from operating in Carmel.

We wandered down the narrow road that snaked towards the sea and discovered a surprising twilight world. Dozens of bonfires glowed across the one-mile long stretch of sand. At first, I thought they were homeless people sleeping by the edge of the Pacific Ocean. But as we got closer, I realised they were families cooking dinner in one of the most picturesque settings I've ever seen, backlit by the soft glow of the sunset.

"Carmel is the Place to Be," as the bumper stickers here say . . .

"Hello mate. You'll never guess where I am."

The voice on the other end of the phone sounded horribly clear and very familiar. I didn't need two guesses to work out our first visitor from Britain had arrived in La La Land,

and seemed to be expecting bed and breakfast.

But there is one big draw back for anyone who decides to descend on us – four children whose sleeping habits mean a dawn chorus of screaming and fighting virtually every morning. Since my friend – we'll call him Chummy – is one of life's eternal bachelors whose idea of a good time is staying out until 5am and then getting up around lunchtime, I could sense trouble on the horizon.

"I'm at the airport. Any chance of popping out to pick me up?"

My heart sank. I toyed with the idea of telling him to hire a car at LAX, Los Angeles' international airport, then I would not have to drop him back there for his departure.

But an hour later, I was driving back towards Brentwood with Chummy chattering enthusiastically about how marvellous life was in London. (Why is it that friends in Britain seem obsessed with telling me this?)

My visitor also had other things on his mind.

"I'd love to get one of those old convertible Mustangs. Why don't we go to that Rent-a-Wreck place?"

My heart sank for the second but not the last time. Every 30 to 45-year-old I know seems to have an obsession about Rent-a-Wreck whenever they visit La La Land. You would think a car hire company that sets out to rent you tatty, rusting heaps would go out of business in a day. Not in the City of Angels.

The Lambourghini Countach you can rent for a modest $750-a-day from Budget in Beverly Hills is rarely hired, but Rent-a-Wreck has become every yuppy's dream. The idea is that it makes you look more like a local if you drive around town in a heap of twisted metal. Some of Hollywood's most famous under-thirtysomethings have even been paying garages good money to cover their own cars in dents as part of this trendy new craze. So next time you see Charlie Sheen driving through town in a dented Porsche, remember that maybe he paid for the damage to be done deliberately...

Not surprisingly, Rent-a-Wreck's old cars do break down from time to time. Then there are their rates. You can hire a safe, secure reliable four-door compact from a "normal" company for the same price as one clapped-out Mustang. In fact, Rent-a-Wreck even hire out new cars themselves. Which surely says it all!

I tried in vain to explain all this to Chummy. But he had his heart set. Thirty minutes later, his off-white Mustang coughed and spluttered as he followed me on the three-mile trip back to my home. In my untrendy Chevy, I couldn't help smiling every time he conked out at traffic lights.

But Chummy did win the kids over the moment he walked through the door by giving them each the biggest bag of candies they had ever seen. His kind and thoughtful gift went down like a lead balloon with mom – who'd just splashed out a small fortune on U.S. dentistry for the entire family.

Determined not to be dragged down by the jet lag, Chummy expected a tour of Hollywood's wildest places within minutes of unpacking his bags. I tried to warn him that the kids would get revenge on him when he was forced out of bed at dawn the next morning...

But at 5.30 am, he discovered for himself that the money saved by staying with friends can never make up for the lack of sleep caused by their children. By ten that very same morning, Chummy had found himself a charming room overlooking the ocean at the picturesque Malibu Beach Inn. I knew then that our friendship would continue.

After a week of joining Chummy most afternoons for a body surf in the Pacific, or a water scooter ride, I realised that guests – even when they don't actually stay in your house – are a very unfortunate diversion. Here I was in Hollywood trying to make it as a script writer and I'd spent a third of my time so far lazing by the beach.

La La Land is full of lost souls who will cheerfully tell you all about the zillions of writing projects they are working on. In most cases they are not being paid for any of them. The sensible lost souls get part-time jobs in restaurants, clubs or shops, but the stupid ones struggle on and eventually fade into oblivion when they run out of savings. I clearly couldn't afford to be one of the latter. And with four kids to support, working in McDonald's wouldn't be lucrative enough. So I supplemented my income by continuing writing as a journalist and author.

Aspiring screenwriters exist here in all types of guises. Take the check-out lady at my local supermarket, The Westward Ho. I'm a regular in this place, partly because it happens to be right next door to Mr Patel the newsagent, and also because Clare loves to get me to pay the week's shopping bill on my credit card whenever the opportunity arises.

This check-out lady's name is Brenda. She's a charming rotund, rosy cheeked person. Always full of the joys of life. I got talking to her one day and she asked me what I did for a living.

"A writer? How wonderful."

She grabbed my arm tightly.

"I've written a screenplay you know."

"Really?" I tried not to sound surprised.

"Yeah," she continued. "It's about a serial killer who comes back from the grave to murder more victims."

I couldn't believe my ears. This neat little grandmotherly figure was trying to be the next Stephen King. Then she asked me the question everyone in Hollywood dreads.

"Would you like to read it?"

"Yes, of course," I lied. What possible use could I be to this dear lady? What she needed was some sharp talking producer. But I looked at her anxious face and realised that it just wouldn't be sensible to try and explain the Hollywood system while ten people were growing impatient waiting in line behind me.

"I'll bring it in next week if you drop by here some time."

"Thanks," I smiled feebly, with an uneasy fear that her ability to write screenplays might far outstretch my own efforts.

A local pizza delivery man has just had his one and only script – entitled *Three Of Hearts* – made into a movie after he forced the screenplay on a top producer he was delivering pizza to in Beverly Hills.

Even the doorman at Twentieth Century Fox tells me he has written six thriller scripts – so far there have been no takers, but who knows? There are about 50,000 screenplays floating around Hollywood at any one time. As the Americans would say, that is truly awesome.

One of the first things I learned within weeks of arriving in La La Land, was that it might be cheaper to live in the U.S. but there are a hell of a lot more things to spend your money on. Take restaurants. Many of them are superb value and well worth recommending. Others – especially in a town like Los Angeles – are vastly overpriced 'pose joints' where those trying to be Hollywood bigwigs attempt to impress their clients (or lovers) by being on first name terms with the Maitre D'.

Initially, we were persuaded to go to these truly awful establishments by certain members of the film industry who just had to be "seen" in places like *The Ivy*, on Robertson Boulevard, in Beverly Hills, and *Chaya*, just around the corner. Avoid these places if you are not a multi-millionaire. There are many more interesting restaurants to visit.

Those pricey joints tend to be full of stiff LA types who have problems making conversation with their bimbo wives/ husbands. On the other hand, if you go to places like the

Cafe Maurice, on La Cienega, you'll get a superb meal, reasonably priced wine and a good atmosphere virtually every night of the week. And it's cheap!

Or visit *The Olive*, on Fairfax. To outside observers this might seem to be an over trendy place. The owners proudly boast that the restaurant's number is not even in the phone book. Well here's the number (213 939 2001) and I highly recommend it. The quality of the food is excellent.

You cannot really live in one of the murder capitals of the world without meeting a... murderer. It's a bit like going to Spain and never eating paella or visiting the Vatican without meeting a Catholic priest.

Anyway, in my part-time capacity as "The Stephen King of True Crime", as my London publisher insists on calling me because of my real-life crime anthologies, I had a legitimate reason for visiting one of La La Land's most notorious killers.

So it was I travelled 250 miles upstate to the charmingly named town of Chowchilla to visit the much feared (and maligned) husband murderess Michele Chapman. Just a few months previously, she had been locked up inside the renowned Central California Women's Facility following the death of her sick and twisted husband.

I had begun communicating by letter with Michele some months earlier after reading about her in the *LA Times*. The case had caught my eye because I could see that she was as much a victim as the man who died at her hands. In fact, if anything, she seemed to be the more wronged of the two parties.

The CCWF is supposed to be one of the most modern top security jails for women in the world. Behind its stark barbed wire fences are some of the most notorious killers in America. As I drove along the perimeter towards the main entrance, pairs of women in regulation jeans and blue shirts strolled casually in the grounds. Opposite the prison, far-mers' combines were peacefully rolling across fields of corn, soyabeans and milo. At the surprisingly unmanned guards' gate, a group of six women inmates were tending to the flower beds. One of them looked up and winked in my direction. I floated by in my tried and trusted Chevy as dark, low-hanging clouds rolled across the southern skies.

My visit inside the CCWF started with a rather severe body search from a well-built shot-putting mother-of-two who had long since forgotten the art of gentle persuasion. Every word was in the form of an order.

"Now your belt."

"What?"

"Your belt. Remove it!"

This was no time to argue, not when dozens of visitors were lining up behind me to do the same thing.

After proving beyond any doubt that I was not trying to smuggle anything other than a few dollar bills inside the CCWF, I proceeded through the electronically operated gates into a no-man's land between the outside and the inside world of more than a thousand hardened criminals.

I stood there while the remote camera zoomed in on my face, no doubt checking for any last moment give away clues as to my real intentions. Then the next gate opened and I found myself inside this "other" world.

I walked about a quarter of a mile to the recreation centre where Michele and forty or so other prisoners were awaiting their much needed visitors.

Ten minutes later Michele Chapman – who kicked her husband to death rather than face any more abuse at his evil hands – was pouring her life out to me. After fifteen years of knocking on people's doors and trying to prise their life's secrets out of them over a cup of tea, it never ceases to amaze me how many people are prepared to do just that.

Michele's story involved the breakdown of a marriage

that had virtually turned into a master-slave scenario... until the day Michele snapped.

Michele enjoyed the opportunity to vent all her old feelings of resentment towards the man who ruined her life. In vivid detail she told me about all the violence and sexual abuse and her struggle to survive. Not once did she stop to wonder why she was telling a perfect stranger such intimate details.

I sat there transfixed as she explained how she was forced into becoming a murderess. Across the room, I suddenly noticed another inmate staring right at me. Michele caught my glance and turned.

"She murdered three successive husbands. They call her the Black Widow."

The woman smiled hazily at me. I made a mental note to avoid any more eye contact.

I couldn't help noticing the four inch heels clipping across the highly polished floor of my local 24-hour supermarket on San Vicente Boulevard. I was crouching at the bottom shelf trying to make up my mind whether to get smooth or crunchy peanut butter at the time. Of such dilemmas is a father-of-four's life made.

The heels seemed to have a mind of their own and I resisted the temptation to glance upwards to their owner in case I found myself at a rather awkward angle in relation to her skirt.

Having solved the peanut problem by getting a jar of smooth and a jar of crunchy to avoid a riot at breakfast the next morning, I re-surfaced and found myself on eye level with an interesting looking dark-haired lady in her mid-thirties, dressed as if she were about to enter a board meeting. She wore a severe, tight-fitting power suit with shoulder pads that would have made an American football star feel proud. We exchanged polite smiles and I headed off for the frozen food department where I was under strict orders to buy a packet of frozen waffles.

Two minutes later I heard the familiar clickety click of those razor sharp stilettos again. She stopped three inches from me and leaned over to take an identical packet of waffles – obviously popular in Brentwood.

A waft of her overpowering perfume hit my nostrils and her cleavage brushed my arm in our desperate scramble for frozen waffles. All this at 9pm on a Sunday evening in a virtually empty supermarket was most puzzling.

"Excuse me," she whispered.

It seemed a reasonable apology considering she had almost knocked me into the seven foot high frozen food compartment. There was a hint of South American in her accent. But maybe I'm just romanticising.

"That's okay," I mumbled, smoothly I hope, before heading for the cash register.

I wasn't in the least surprised that my new best friend in her four-inch heels joined me a few moments later, but I was beginning to suspect this was no ordinary Brentwood housewife. Yet she was also not some starlet dredging the area for a Hollywood player to make her own.

She leaned provocatively against a stack of *National Enquirer* magazines that line the shelves of every self-respecting supermarket check-out area in La La Land, and began to strike up a conversation about how nice Brentwood was. Under the circumstances, I even courteously allowed her to go in front of me in the queue.

I was a bit ruffled by the fact that she waited whilst I paid for my shopping before walking alongside me into the steaming heat of the dark parking lot. Those sharpened heels still clicking happily as we discussed the weather.

"Isn't it great the way the sun shines nearly every day," she enthused. I nodded my head in polite agreement.

Then I felt her perfectly manicured fingernails grab the

top of my arm.

"May I ask you something?"

"Sure."

"I'm a bit short of money at the moment. Would you like to come back to my apartment?"

Her apartment?

"It's awfully nice of you to offer..."

Then it dawned on me. How could I be so naive?

"I'll only charge you $200."

I shook my head, but couldn't help smiling.

"Oh well. It was worth asking..."

Perhaps rather fortunately I never did bump into Miss Four Inch Heels again in my local supermarket. Only in La La Land...

In the middle of September the children were due to start at their new school. Having arrived in early August, we had avoided the school issue for six weeks, but now it was time for them to take their biggest step in terms of adjusting to life in La La Land.

I was well aware of the problems of schooling in the inner cities of the U.S. (and in Britain too for that matter, which has more than its fair share). Before moving to La La Land, a U.S. friend had told me that he had sent his three kids to the local public (free) school in LA, only to discover to his horror that his 12-year-old son's class mates were pushing crack at the back of the playground each day. Understandably, this made us cautious.

In addition, the attraction of a free school system for every child aged between 5 and 18 is heavily outweighed by the fact that, according to reports, many of the inner city children who do not graduate from high school can barely read and seem to know little about the world. In a recent six-nation survey of schoolchildren's mathematics and science skills, U.S. schools scored last in both subjects.

34

This country's public school system seems to be in dire need of restructuring. Thanks to the school busing system that saw students transported out of one neighbourhood and into another to balance racial groups, many middle class people have moved to other areas or started sending their kids to private schools.

E.D. Hirsch, Jr, author of the bestselling book *Cultural Literacy*, writes: "This nation is in peril because students are no longer being taught the shared information that bonds." Hirsch reckons that of the two-thirds of the population who are literate, most of these are at a lower than acceptable level.

The even more ominous problems of discipline within the Los Angeles school system were tragically illustrated in a recent incident at the Fairfax High School, in West Hollywood, a supposedly gang-free neighbourhood, when a 16-year-old student was shot dead after a gun in a fellow student's rucksack went off by accident.

With all this in mind, I knew that if I could scrape together enough money then private schooling was preferable. In London, we had managed to put all our kids through the Lycee Francais Charles de Gaulle, in South Kensington. Each child was bi-lingual by the age of six. This French school system has been set up in many of the world's major cities, including Los Angeles. Most importantly, it was half the cost of other private schools. So our move to La La Land became all the more easy because the children entered a school system identical to the one they had just left.

That first day, I found myself in a mile-long traffic jam of Porsches and Mercedes at the entrance to the Lycee de Los Angeles' winding hilly drive. This was the place that proudly boasted it had educated Jodie Foster and "many other famous Hollywood stars". The school is situated in an area called Cheviot Hills, just around the corner from the site of one of the most notorious Hollywood murders of all time; former Playboy bunny Dorothy Stratten was gunned down by her jealous ex-hubby who was promptly arrested amid rumours of a scandalous relationship with a famous movie director. This makes Cheviot Hills an area of historical significance, according to the *LA Times*.

The first day at school went off without incident and so it has continued. Unlike the Lycee in London, this school is filled with a vast ethnic mix, which the children love. They were particularly impressed with the fact that some pupils take sushi to school in their lunchboxes. One little boy is so fond of raw fish his nanny has to pick up the sushi from an early morning restaurant en route to school.

Not surprisingly, the appearance of a piece of rather foul smelling raw fish lying stone cold dead in his lunchbox was a sight that most of the other children in his class grew to dread. I personally took it upon myself to convince my children that sushi was not something I wished to encourage. Thankfully, they were much happier with a ham sandwich and a packet of chips (that's crisps to you and me).

The biggest problem came a few weeks into term when Polly announced she no longer wished to be dropped off outside the school because she was ashamed of my beloved Chevy. The other kids teased her mercilessly about it and she insisted that I drop her two hundred yards from the school entrance rather than be seen in my "dreadful" car.

Around the end of September, Clare and I arranged to meet a couple of friends for a drink right in the middle of Beverly Hills. The pavements of Rodeo Drive and Crescent Drive might well be paved with gold if you tend to dress in Georgio Armani suits, but if you're a scruffy Brit in a pair of shorts it's better to steer clear of such areas.

Everything is at a premium in Beverly Hills, the rents, the shops, even the car parking charges. Recently, a parking control officer, as they're called out here, insisted that he had not been insensitive in ticketing a corpse! He claimed he had been threatened so many times in the past by irate motorists that he had a habit of slapping tickets on windscreens and then moving on as fast as possible. The case got quite a lot of coverage in the newspapers and local TV. I never could quite fathom out whether the media coverage was a result of genuine outrage over the warden's insensitivity, or just plain amusement at the fact he had given a motorist a ticket without noticing he was dead!

But more important for me, the bars are at a premium in Beverly Hills. Drinking can be horrendously expensive. Take the bar/restaurant *Tribeca* as a classic example. This is basically a millionaire singles club where dinner for two sets you back a sizeable sum and more often than not you can find yourself sitting near a billionaire inventor of the collapsable coat hanger who has just married a walking X-ray, forty years his junior.

Having discovered this, we quickly left the *Tribeca* and headed across the street to the world famous Beverly Wilshire Hotel (where the film *Pretty Woman* was located). This was not a good move. When the drinks bill was placed under my nose by a rather snotty waiter, I knew I should have kept to my own favourite type of $2-a-head watering hole. $10 per glass and they didn't even give us peanuts to munch on. Places like the Beverly Wilshire are for people on business expense accounts. It's a charming hotel filled with nervous people trying to work out if they can spot someone famous in the lobby.

After a mortgageable round of drinks, we shot out of the hotel back onto Wilshire Boulevard and found ourselves desperately looking for somewhere warm and cosy. I spotted a crowd of people milling around what looked like a bar entrance and confidently, if unwittingly, led our party into the depths of Beverly Hills most tacky nightclub.

Little did I know this was *Stringfellows* – a place I had

studiously avoided for ten years in London. Now, a few weeks after arriving in tinseltown, I was breaking the habit of a lifetime.

During my stint as a reporter in London, *Stringfellows* was one of those establishments where Page Three Girls exercised their hips and orange-skinned men with green-tinted blond footballers' hair styles tried to sell you second-hand XR3s.

Back in Beverly Hills, I walked through the teeming masses of American equivalents of Sharons and Rons towards the bar before I noticed the gaudy neon sign sprawled above the bar.

Two hard, round things suddenly pushed into my back like concrete footballs. As I turned, a woman in her early twenties with perfectly capped teeth glinted a smile in my direction like something out of a toothpaste commercial. The "things" pressing into my back were her ample bosoms, as they used to say in London in the fifties. As I leaned back I felt the full force of them once more – they were obviously manufactured out of pure silicone. I had just encountered my first rebuilt Beverly Hills *babe*.

Hemmed in by a sea of even more silicone as tight-fitting dress after tight-fitting dress squeezed past me, I struggled to find a route through the plastic. These girls were mighty proud of their busts. By the time I reached Clare and the others, I was in danger of becoming a silicone junkie.

Of the nation's 200,000 breast implant operations in 1991, Californians accounted for over 45,000, according to the American Society of Plastic and Reconstructive Surgeons.

It was around this time that I decided there was one important aspect of life in Los Angeles that I had to 'take on board' – getting fit. Over the previous two or three years I had become disgracefully unhealthy and watching all those lean muscled men and women pounding the tarmac on the busy San Vicente thoroughfare near my home made me realise that perhaps I should consider getting in shape.

In a recent newspaper survey it was revealed that two out of three Los Angeles residents run the equivalent of at least one mile every day. Most mornings there are wave upon wave of lycra-skinned joggers pounding the blacktops of La La Land. A girl I know who works as vice president of movie development at a major studio (it sounds impressive but her salary is modest and there are 90 VPs at that particular studio), gets up at 6am every morning so she can work out for two hours before getting to the office. No wonder one visitor to the City of Angels recently commented: "Los Angeles must be the only place on earth where people arrive at work more exhausted than when they left the previous day . . ."

Anyway, if you are going to jog, then San Vicente Boulevard is probably the perfect place; pink flowering coral trees line a wide island of grass that runs all the way down the centre of the road to Santa Monica, three miles away. Some Hollywood folk reckon more early morning deals are signed and sealed during a run on San Vicente than at the biggest studios in town. And I for one was definitely in need of a deal. So, with all this in mind, I made the momentous decision to go jogging.

My first big mistake was to announce my intentions to the rest of the family. They immediately wanted a piece of the action.

"But you can't all come."

This was not what I had in mind at all, pounding the pavements of Brentwood, knocking every living soul out of our paths like some juvenile gang of wannabe keep fitters.

Luckily they didn't all last the course and after a barrage of complaints about wanting to go to the loo we were down to two; only my four-year-old and I were powering our way to peak fitness.

The sun had just started its descent into the Pacific ahead of us when a rather odd looking individual in an orange tinted toupee and smoking a fat cigar started running alongside. I took no notice at first. But then as the pungent smoke of his cigar overwhelmed me, I turned to him in irritation. He took this as a sign of encouragement and smiled cheerily.

"That your kid?" he said, nodding towards Fergus. "Cute kid."

His purple lycra bicycle shorts were far too loud and obvious for him to be some would-be paedophile – unfortunately, Brentwood's male residents seem to lean towards the skin tight, balls-round-your-ankles look – but you can never be too sure.

I gasped between alternate clouds of cigar smoke and smog, while he continued singing the praises of my four-year-old, who was sprinting ten yards ahead of me like some fully trained Olympic athlete.

"Can he act?"

I gave him a withering look. Why the hell couldn't he jog elsewhere?

"I'm a producer. Give me a call sometime and we'll screen test him."

Oh yeah, I thought, trying vainly to outrun him. Dammit! He was older than me!

At that moment, our 'Hollywood Bigwig' nearly lost his toupée when a gust of wind threatened to dump it in a nearby garden. Without stopping, he managed to adjust his hair, manoeuvre his business card from his anorak pocket before overtaking me and speeding off into the smoggy sunset. Feeling an unfit failure, I dumped the card in the nearest trash can.

Within another few minutes we were jaded, exhausted and desperate to find the quickest route home. Just then I noticed a rather gaudy yellow Rolls Royce with chauffeur pull up on the opposite side of the road. Seconds later, Mr Hollywood Bigwig jogged up and jumped in the back seat, still puffing out vast clouds of cigar smoke. I immediately altered our course and headed back towards that trash can, but I never managed to find his card. Maybe I should learn to take people in this town more seriously...

OCTOBER

This whole town operates in a dance of seduction.
Linda Buzzell

The screams were ear piercing. Long screeching cries for help that seemed never ending.

And I knew that they were coming from at least two of my children.

I struggled to open the French doors and rushed into the back garden. The pool was filled with red clouds of what could only be blood and the unmistakable shape of a shark's fin was cutting the surface...

I awoke with a start. Another nightmare. Ever since we had touched down in La La Land, I had been suffering from vivid nightmares that could only be destroyed by forcing myself to wake up. Perhaps Los Angeles' thousands of psychologists would interpret these dreams as some deep set fear and loathing for the City of Angels. And admittedly, I had felt very worried about transplanting ourselves to a foreign land.

It was still dark outside. I lay breathing heavily, trying to relax, but somewhere in my subconscious I was sure that I really had heard a screeching sound too real to be part of a dream. I strained my ears, but the only sound was the whistling of the Santa Ana winds in the huge oak tree twenty feet from the front door.

I was just starting to drift back to sleep when an ear piercing scream came from the garden. I leaped out of bed and peered through the curtains. Outside, the night looked deathly still. Suddenly, the dustbin in the alleyway toppled

43

over with a loud clang. Now I was seriously spooked.

Outside, the eerie silence returned.

Bravely I tried to persuade Clare to investigate, but when this was met with indignant grunts I put on my Marks and Sparks towelling robe and crept quietly through the house, careful not to wake the children.

I was inching open the front door, when I realised I had nothing to protect myself with against this intruder. For the first time during our stay in La La Land, I envied the British couple we knew who were so paranoid about being robbed, they had both taken expert firearms tuition at $50 an hour at the Beverly Hills Gun Club and then planted a total of six deadly weapons in strategic places around their house in the Hollywood Hills.

Anyone can own a gun here. Parts of the state are as sparsely populated and cut off from civilisation as many areas of the Sahara Desert. In these places, the gun rules and pick-up trucks with rifles strapped in the back windows are a common sight. There is a law against concealing a weapon. That means it is illegal to carry a loaded weapon in the glove-box of your car, for example. But there is nothing illegal about having a gun in one pocket and bullets in the other. An estimated three million trigger happy people – including at least 100,000 Brits – are merrily wandering around this city armed to the teeth. But not me...

Back in quiet, respectable, safe Brentwood that night, I grabbed my four-year-old's miniature baseball bat that happened to be lying on the hall table. Slowly, I eased open the front door and felt the warm night breeze whistling around my ankles.

My eyes panned across the dark lawn. Nothing. Not a thing. I stepped gingerly out onto the pathway. There was a definite rustling sound over by the oak tree. Someone was there. Instinctively, I let out a growl, well, more like a long grunt.

But my intruder did not move from his hiding place. My nerves were now seriously frayed, but dressed in a bright red dressing gown and carrying a toy baseball bat, I continued my search and destroy mission by slowly moving towards the tree. I could now hear heavy breathing. I was trying not to think about what I was going to do when I confronted the intruder.

Another rustle. I looked down and saw Bubbles our friendly, south west London cat looking as scared as I was. She was glued to the spot, hair on end, and obviously very distressed. Half of her tail was hanging limply.

For a few seconds I thought she'd been attacked by one of these evil satanist gangs that the local TV news is always warning us to be on the lookout for. Apparently, they specialise in cutting up domestic cats and sacrificing them to the devil around Halloween. But this was only the first week in October and Halloween was nearly a month away.

Suddenly, there was a sinister hiss from the blackness. My hair stood on end just like the cat's. As I turned, a pair of red glinting eyes stared at me from the darkness. I inched closer and saw the outline of a weird looking dog. Or was it a fox?

It growled. I stepped back. I growled. The creature looked at me mystified for a moment, then turned and casually sauntered off into the darkness.

Bubbles and I had just encountered our first coyote. As we made a swift retreat towards the safety of the house, I heard something behind me. The coyote was back and fast approaching. I slammed the door shut just before our new best friend managed to join us.

"Don't worry. They're harmless old boy. Actually, they make rather good pets," one of my British friends told me a few days later.

Coyotes aren't the only animals that live in the hills behind Brentwood. Rabid skunks, mangy possums and a large selection of poisonous snakes are among our residents. Bubbles has even had a close shave with a lynx. I'm sure the poor creature must long for her relatively charmed life in Parson's Green.

But it could have been worse. I might have ended up having to attend a pet grief therapy programme where heartbroken pet owners go after losing their loved ones. Apparently La La Land has at least 100,000 such bereaving citizens at any one time and, naturally, many of them feel obliged to seek out the expert help of psychotherapists like Diane Kelley who specialises in counselling clients who have just lost their furry friends.

"Such a loss can have a drastic impact on a pet owner's life. It can be as devastating as losing any other member of your family," she says with great earnest.

Meeting the wild dogs of the Brentwood Hills made us suddenly realise that we were living in a city that was nothing more than a strip of desert less than a hundred years ago.

Without the millions of gallons of water that pour every day onto each plant and strip of grass in the place, La La Land would turn back into desert within a short space of time. LA is constantly facing drought problems, yet sprinkler systems, swimming pools and just about every recreational activity relies on water. Latest figures claim there are more than a million pools in the city!

In the second week of October we decided to host a dinner party for some of the new friends we had made since arriving in La La Land.

Few La La Landers host dinner parties at home. Many prefer to wine and dine their guests in restaurants. Not realising this, I had been deeply embarrassed when, only a few weeks earlier, we were asked out by a couple and three friends of ours tagged along.

At the end of the meal, the man who had invited us out grabbed the bill and insisted on paying. He saw it as a matter of pride that he should pay, even though I was fully expecting to go dutch. The total cost was a whopping $400 but he inissted it was their treat because they had asked us out.

We, on the other hand, could neither afford nor wished to host a meal at the local rip-off joint, so we sat down one evening and decided which people in La La Land would be most fun to invite to a dinner party. It was not an easy task.

"They'll never get on," I said when my wife suggested one slightly stuffy couple. "They don't drink. They don't smoke. Ask them around another day – preferably when I'm not here."

The next problem was the food and drink. Clare made a dawn raid on the local farmers' market, on Third Street, in the centre of Santa Monica, a city on the western edge of Los Angeles where it sometimes seems as if every other person you meet is British. Early morning at the market – which is only held on Wednesdays – is a bit like visiting one of those bustling, colourful fruit and vegetable market squares in Provence.

But it's the prices at the Santa Monica market that are the biggest attraction. Juicy, ripe plum tomatoes for as little as a buck for six. Twelve succulent oranges for under two bucks. Huge cartons of rosy red strawberries. Bunches of poppies and other flowers by the dozen. Even cappuccino stalls. The market makes you realise just how cheaply you can live in La La Land.

As Clare toured the market, I was dispatched to buy drink from a store that one friend told me had the "cheapest booze in all of LA."

Trader Joe's is a chain of shops that specialises in bulk buying. Scattered around the city, they have forsaken shelves and signs for good old fashioned value. And some of their prices are an affront to healthy profit margins.

Within seconds of grabbing a shopping cart and marching into Trader Joe's on National Boulevard, near the junction with Westwood Boulevard, I was stocking up with caseloads of booze that would have put me into serious debt back in Britain. First, the beer. I picked the cheapest amber nectar called *Chihuaha*, which is basically Corona beer with a different label. Imported from across the border in Mexico, it's light in colour but strong in flavour. But most important of all, it costs the equivalent of 40 pence a bottle!

Then I headed for the wines and picked up a great little Chianti for $3.99 a bottle plus some Californian Chardonnay for just $3.39. I used to turn my nose up at Californian wines when we lived in Britain. Now, with the temperature permanently in the seventies or above, there's nothing better than a crisp, icy glass of Californian Chardonnay. One hour later, I had parted with less than fifty pounds for 24 bottles of wine and three crates of beer.

And so we were ready for our first La La Land dinner party. It began inauspiciously. The problem with people in the film industry is that most of them only want to talk about themselves. I have frequently sat next to so-called movie icons who never even asked me what I did for a living, but happily spent three hours describing in minute detail the technical importance of video post-production.

Our guests included a hunky, former American TV soap star and his serious wife, complete with her best friend who was a blonde and statuesque Australian producer, a scatty but sweet wardrobe girl whose boyfriend was away on a film shoot, a film director who wanted to be the next David Lean but had to make do with car commercials, and an eccentric little Charlie Drake-type who'd left London for the golden pavements of LA because no-one in the British film industry appreciated his talents.

For the first two hours little or no conversation was exchanged. The people who knew each other talked amongst themselves and the rest struggled to mumble the most basic pleasantries. By 10.30, I was ready to wrap the entire disastrous evening up and sweep everyone out of the door, but just then, our soap star spotted something behind my right shoulder.

"That's not a bottle of Tequila is it?"

After two hours of watching people sip sedately at their glasses of wine, I grabbed the bottle and virtually forced a glass down his throat.

An Australian voice came from across the table,

"Oh Tequila. I'd love some."

"Got any champagne to go with it? Sparkling wine will do if you haven't." Our would-be David Lean was suggesting a lethal slammer – a combination of Tequila and champagne. The tall blonde's eyes lit up.

Half an hour later, everyone on that table had consumed at least three Tequila slammers. For those of you who don't know what a slammer is, here's a brief description: you pour a decent sized dollop of Tequila into a glass and then follow it with an equal measure of something sparkling. Champagne is best. Then cover the top of the glass with a cloth and slam it down as hard as possible on the table. The gasses mix with the Tequila to form pure alcoholic froth and at that point you should down the entire contents in one gulp. Anyone who doesn't is a cissy. The effect is similar to what happens when the dentist gives you a pain-killing shot. In seconds you're in cloud cuckoo land.

Nine fully grown, responsible adults, with at least a dozen children between them, had just proved that Tequila slammers do work. Everyone was completely smashed. Alcohol can break down the highest barriers. These people who would not have said boo to a goose an hour earlier were now chattering enthusiastically about all sorts of subjects. And my soap hero was leading the way in every respect.

"Anyone fancy a swim," he yelled at the top of his voice.

A few seconds later, David Lean and Charlie Drake were prancing out towards the pool followed closely by our two sporting maidens, as my back garden turned into one of those happy smiling scenes from *Health and Efficiency* magazine.

First to strip off was the tall Australian producer, followed swiftly by the wardrobe girl who shed her own wardrobe like a real professional. David Lean and Charlie Drake joined in the fun, even though they were both definitely in need of a few months down at the gym.

But we had all ignored one very important factor: overlooking this noisy skinny dipping session were the bedrooms of our three youngest children.

Suddenly a window banged open and an indignant eleven-year-old voice screamed: "Get your clothes on you disgraceful woman."

The voices of two other highly irritated children joined in the protest.

"That is disgusting. I cannot believe you are allowing them to do this."

"Daddy. Don't you dare look."

Children seem to have a pretty straight-laced view of life. In the end, my kids won the day and all my naked dinner guests retired tail between their legs (in a manner of speaking) and put on their clothes before returning to their safe, well, insecure sort of lives in the movie industry.

The neighbours in our little street in Brentwood were a mixed bunch. There was a very wealthy doctor next door who owned a selection of eight different Mercedes. Opposite was a wily old woman who felt she had something in common with us because her son lived in Weybridge, Surrey.

"If you're from England you must know him," she insisted.

Then there was the brat from hell, whose parents never

bothered to check us out, even though he used to haunt our front garden, playing with my youngest in the street outside.

And finally, there was the little old lady who lived right next door to us. She seemed as bright as a button when she came knocking on our door one day asking if I could help her repair a faulty light in her car. With a mop of bright red hair and a rather endearing pixy face she looked like everyone's ideal granny.

The car in question was a thirty year old Dodge Dart, which had driven all of ten thousand miles since new. In La La Land, people often keep their cars for thirty or even forty years. They get them serviced every six months and there are no problems with rust. It's pleasant to see all these vintage cars floating around the city. The mechanic at my local garage has an immaculate Thunderbird that he bought the year of my birth – 1956 – for $2,000. It's probably worth $50,000 now, but he won't part with it until the day he dies.

Back at the little old lady's house that afternoon, she explained to me what the problem was.

"Look. Whenever I open the trunk I can see the light is still on. It will not go off."

I tried to explain that all trunk lights come on when you open the trunk. But she was adamant.

A few days later I began to realise that maybe all was not well with our little old lady.

"Oh. Have you just moved in next door?" she asked me with obviously no recollection of our car boot conference a few days earlier.

"I'm having a problem getting my car started. Would you mind having a look at it?"

Again I followed her into her neat little Hansel and Gretel home. Two minutes later, I established that she was trying to put the key the wrong way in the ignition.

The end of October was marked by Halloween. In America,

the ghouls of Halloween have been turned into a billion dollar business. On the last day of October every year the whole country seems obsessed by dead bodies, vampires and witches. My kids were swept up by it all – they even wore fancy dress to school. The outfits would have horrified any English child psychiatrist.

My four-year-old sported an outfit that consisted of a rubber monster mask with a knife sticking out each side and fake blood smothered all over his face. The two girls were slightly more conservative in their choices; one wore a surgeon's green overall covered in fake innards while the other decided a walking skeleton looked nicest.

But the day before Halloween, thirteen-year-old Toby surpassed all this by announcing that we should go shopping for a human skull at a trendy new shop called *Necromance* on Melrose Avenue, the equivalent of King's Road, Chelsea. He dragged me into the store and made me look at delicacies such as a stuffed two-headed kitten, ear-rings made out of human bone, human fingers on a leather cord, dangling skunk jaws and chicken vertebrae for a bargain $12. Apparently, every self-respecting heavy metal merchant in town shops at this store whenever he wants to buy a birthday present for the girl of his dreams.

Nancy Smith, who runs the shop and looks like Cruella De Vil's daughter, goes by the nicknames Necro Nancy and the Bone Lady. She proudly told me that she had just sold a pickled iguana to an Oscar winning actor. She defended her business passionately.

"People think bones mean murder. They don't. They're part of a science, a decoding of the mysteries of the past."

Oh really Nancy...

Just then a housewifely type in a red knitted dress walked up and boldly enquired about a human foetus.

"It's not for me, it's for my husband. His father made him throw one out when he was a kid and he's longed for another ever since," she explained earnestly to Nancy.

"We're not allowed to stock them. You have to make a formal request to the nearest medical school. They might help," a very straight-faced Necro Nancy told her.

I managed to dissuade Toby from buying anything after we had a little chat about the intricate ins and outs of taxidermy.

"I think I'll just get a George Bush mask," he volunteered. I had no doubt that would be far more frightening.

The next part of this Halloween tradition – sparked off three hundred years ago by a group of devil worshippers in Salem, Massachusetts – was to visit a haunted house.

I kept thinking about one particular gruesome headline in the *LA Times* a few days earlier that had proclaimed: "Aborted Foetuses Used In Haunted House."

Apparently, some rather over enthusiastic Halloween fans had staged a haunted house in a church in San Diego and decided to use real foetuses to "entertain" innocent families. The nutty pastor who ran the whole horror show told the paper: "We used the haunted house as a tool. These are real issues in life, and they have to be addressed." Sometimes I wish Californians did not take things so seriously.

Later that Halloween evening, all six of us queued in an orderly fashion outside a rather dark and dingy looking building that had a sign saying: "Haunted House". It was $2 a head, which seemed a bit steep just to walk around the local youth club, but the children were most insistent.

The double doors finally opened and we began the "trip of a lifetime", as the teenager shelling out the tickets described it. Within seconds, my four-year-old was clinging to my trouser leg for dear life and my nine-year-old was close to tears.

The first room was the hanging room. Four authentic looking bodies were strung up from the ceiling, their faces gruesome. Now I knew where all those countless horror movies got their make-up artists. Most of them trained as children every Halloween at the Brentwood Youth Club.

The next dungeon was even more horrific. A decapitated head swung out of nowhere and we had to duck to avoid it squelching into our faces. Four-year-old Fergus was in complete hysterics by now. Continual spooky noises were coming from a state-of-the-art stereo system. My kids were scared out of their tiny minds, but incredibly there were even some parents in this shop of horrors with babies and toddlers. I heard one dad discussing every gory detail of a body with his infant.

The climax of this gruesome exhibition was a coffin with an aspiring Freddy Krueger dressed head to toe in bandages who appeared to be auditioning for *Nightmare on Elm Street 99*.

A few minutes later I emerged from the youth club-come-morgue with three kids close to nervous breakdowns and a complete bewilderment with the Americans over their obsession with Halloween. It had cost me at least $200 in fancy dress outfits alone. Still to come was the trick or treating – an age old Halloween tradition that probably does more to encourage paedophiles with aspirations to become child killers, than anything else in this weird and wonderful society. Essentially, your children risk life and limb by knocking on as many strangers' doors as possible and yelling, "Trick or Treat", in order to be rewarded with a handful of candies that will either rot their expensive teeth or kill them within seconds.

In the past few years there has been an increasingly large number of incidents in La La Land that suggest not everyone believes in the neighbourly spirit of Halloween. A popular past-time for bored child-haters is to place razor blades inside bars of chocolate. Other pleasant souls are fond of mixing laxative pills with the candies.

With all these horror stories ringing in my ears, I wasn't exactly keen for my tribe to hit the streets of La La Land.

"But everyone does it here," protested Rosie.

"All our school friends are doing it, so why can't we?" another indignant voice asked.

First port of call was the little old lady from next door. I doubted whether she would even realise it was Halloween.

But her senile dementia had taken a vacation and she was buzzing with ghoulish Halloween spirit. As she poured handfuls of sweets into each of the kids' bags, she turned to me and said: "You're new in the street aren't you?".

Next stop was a house that looked like a one-storey version of the mansion out of the *Addams Family*. There was no light on as we fought our way through the wild overgrowth you normally find in the jungles of Borneo.

When I pressed the door bell, it didn't so much ring as crackle. We all stood in silence. There was no movement from the house.

"Press harder Daddy."

Rosie had already started tucking into her feast of free sweets and was determined to replenish supplies as swiftly as possible. I rang the bell again.

A torch light suddenly swept across the garden, but as we turned, the light disappeared inside the house. Whoever was there did not want to open the door to us. I motioned to the children to retreat hastily.

But as I tried to take command of my troops, the front door creaked open slowly. We froze in our tracks.

"What do you want?" asked an old, slow, menacing voice.

The door opened wider to reveal a gaunt woman in a black cape with a hood. I was starting to get a bad feeling about this place. The kids were so scared they forgot to say trick or treat.

Then the door opened wider and three midgets covered in green paint and each with a knife through their head jumped out. For a few moments we were all glued to the spot. Then the midgets screamed: "Trick or Treat!"

This was a family who took its Halloween duties deadly seriously. All five of us hurried back to the relative safety of the street. The witch called after us: "Don't you want any candies?"

Not even my eleven-year-old would turn back.

A few days later, I read the newspaper reports of the Halloween celebrations. The good old *LA Times* pronounced: "Halloween Mostly Peaceful in L.A. Area."

Buried at the end of this short account of the festivities was the following revelation: A noisy house party in the Antelope Valley turned violent when a large contingent of Los Angeles County sheriff's deputies arrived to quiet the Littlerock gathering.

"One party-goer, incensed that the band had stopped playing, pulled out a handgun and fired at the musicians to get them to resume, authorities said."

So that counts as a "peaceful" Halloween in La La Land . . .

NOVEMBER

*All of us are in the gutter but some of us are
looking up at the stars.*
Oscar Wilde

"Daddy. Why has the tree had a haircut?"

My four-year-old son Fergus has a great way of putting things. Autumn was here. The huge oak tree in the garden was bare. The days were shorter. But still the temperatures crept into the eighties. La La Land doesn't really have seasons in the normally accepted sense of the word. Most days I would wake up around 6.30 and feel a cold dampness in the air as I walked up the garden path to pick up the seven tons of newsprint which goes by the name *Los Angeles Times*.

Clouds of low-lying mist would often shroud the garden like the set of a Hollywood horror movie. At that time of the morning, it could feel like a typical November day back in Britain.

But by 9am, all my nostalgia would have disappeared along with the early morning mist as temperatures soared and I would find myself in the middle of warm sunshine that would have attracted tens of thousands to Brighton beach on any summer's day.

Our friendly *mailperson* – an Ella Fitzgerald look-alike – treated every day of the year the same in La La Land. That meant she wore the blue Bermuda shorts that seem to be a permanent part of the uniform of the United States Postal Service here and she was always singing Ray Charles' greatest hits.

In La La Land – and most parts of the U.S. for that

matter – there is a mailbox at the end of every garden where letters are deposited and picked up by the mailperson. Ella used to show up most mornings in her dinky little postal service jeep, specially manufactured with left-hand drive so that she did not have to get out of the vehicle when dropping off the post. But Ella was a friendly old soul and she often preferred to sling her jeep up on the sidewalk and visit each house on her two feet – walking is a rare skill in La La Land. No doubt the efficiency experts back at headquarters would have been horrified, but then no-one in our little street was going to tell on Ella. With her round friendly face and beautifully plaited hair, she looked more like a police officer directing traffic in Barbados than a Los Angeles postwoman.

But it was her false finger nails that fascinated Clare and I. They must have measured at least three inches in length and they curved inwards as if she was in possession of some magical powers and a brass lantern.

One day my wife asked Ella how on earth she managed to stop her falsies from snapping in two on her rounds of the tree-lined streets of Brentwood.

"Super glue," she replied without blinking.

"In any case they come in real handy when I want to open the mail in a hurry. Here, let me show you..."

With that, Ella grabbed the letters she had just handed to us on the doorstep, pierced one particularly well-sealed buff envelope and ripped it open in a split second.

"See. Easy as pie when you know how."

We laughed nervously. I wondered how Ella's husband coped with those finger nails at night. The mind boggled.

Now that the season in La La Land was changing, we got to thinking about the sort of locations that would make ideal settings for November weekend breaks.

And the inspiration for our next jaunt came during a rather tedious lunch at the executive canteen in Paramount

Studios. A producer was wining and dining me with a view to giving me a writing assignment when we started talking about some of the great places to visit near La La Land.

Until this point, my attention had been flagging. The main problem with this particular chap was that he had become so caught up in the corporate structure of the studio that he couldn't take a mouthful of his food without glancing over my shoulder at the Hollywood players drifting by after their traditional movie executive's lunch of a dry salad and mineral water.

"Oh there's Brandon. We played tennis last week," he told me proudly. I gazed blankly at the tennis-playing Brandon, which I suspect was not the appropriate reaction. I'd already upset this producer by asking for wine with the meal and when I began munching on the bread rolls before our Gazpacho even showed up, I think he gave up on me and put me firmly into the Hollywood category of heavy eater and drinker with an attitude problem.

Basically, there are four main rules to abide by if a top producer decides to buy you lunch at a studio restaurant:

One: The Arrival

Be as conspicuous as possible when you walk in. Preferably, try to find at least five people at other tables to greet before you even get to your host. Sometimes, it's rather effective to stand at the reception area and just cast your eyes around the restaurant to spot any faces. It's not so easy to see people as you are walking through a crowded place – and there's always the risk you might trip over if you don't watch where you are going.

Two: The Greeting

If you are meeting a female then only kiss them on one side of the cheek. La La Land women cannot cope with the French style two-kiss. One or two believe they are more likely to get AIDS that way! If it's a man you're greeting then try not to shake his hand in the traditional Anglo Saxon

59

way. A trendy homeboy-style slap of palms has now become accepted practise in Hollywood.

Three: The Conversation

No Hollywood executive is interested in whether you're married or have children (or both!). In fact, I've given up trying to explain to astonished La La Landers that I'm married with four children, by the same woman. ("Wow!" is usually their only reply). Conversation usually cartwheels straight into talking about the latest film releases. The idea is that this executive will get an idea of *where you're coming from* if he interrogates you about recent movies. If you condemn a transvestite serial killer psychological thriller as "a load of nonsense" and he or she likes it, then you're unlikely to get any work from them.

Four: Table Manners

Always leave your Ray Bans around your neck. It's not cool to put them on the table – and you might forget them anyway. Smoking is a non-starter. If you meet a movie executive who smokes then you might as well walk away there and then because he definitely could not be employed at any of the major studios. Never finish the food on your plate. Health conscious Hollywood players always leave a few morsels because it shows they are non-reliant people with no compulsions. The truth is that most of them have just come out of Alcoholics Anonymous, Narcotics Anonymous or Sex Anonymous.

By the time you've remembered all this there is little room for any real conversation. So that was why it was a relief to talk about interesting places to visit in California with my producer friend from Paramount rather than negative pick-ups and gross takings.

"What's Palm Springs like?"

"You haven't been to Palm Springs?"

The whole of California has an upsetting habit of answering a question with a question. I once asked a guy what he did for a job. He replied: "I work in Real Estate?" I have even stopped on Melrose Avenue to ask a cop directions and he's said: "You go right at McDonald's?" Hang on! Are you telling me or asking me?

Meanwhile, back to Palm Springs.

"Can you recommend a hotel?"

"Hotel?" Here we go again. "There are hundreds of hotels in Palm Springs but we always stay at Melanie's father's ranch."

I made a mental note to make sure I avoided any ranchers with producer sons-in-law when I got to Palm Springs.

When the waiter brought the check, I sighed with relief as my Paramount friend insisted on paying. You can never be too sure in a place like Hollywood. There's one British producer I know who has asked me out for lunch on three occasions, and each time claimed he has forgotten his wallet at the end of the meal, leaving me to foot the bill. The last time he called me, I gently reminded him to remember his wallet. I haven't heard from him since.

So, with the producer from hell's description of Palm Springs ringing in my ears, I returned home and decided to organise a romantic night away from screaming kids, in a town made famous by Frank Sinatra and George Burns and Bob Hope, whose combined ages total about 300 years (if they're still alive by the time you read this).

A few days later, I was waiting at the entrance to the 405 freeway in an inevitable line of traffic before heading for Palm Springs, when a figure approached me. The first thing I noticed about him was the makeshift belt holding up his pants. It was bright yellow plastic law enforcement tape and read: "Caution – Do Not Cross Line."

I had long since stopped being surprised by the vast number of homeless people out on the streets of La La Land. The United States may be the world's richest country, but an estimated 500,000 of its citizens spend their days not knowing where they are going to spend their nights.

There is apparently a National Hobo Association that meets every month in a youth club in Beverly Hills. At its last gathering, it recommended to members that those suffering from haemorrhoid problems should use rubber doughnuts to sleep on!

Clare and the children are always giving pan handlers a dollar. But I'm more cautious. It's difficult to be sympathetic with their plight when they're wearing gleaming new trainers complete with a shell suit, which is often the case, holding up cardboard signs that have become a virtual LA art-form in themselves:

"Tired of Beans. Will work for peanuts."

"Needy not Greedy"

"Anything is Better than Nothing."

However, this particular character coming towards me was clearly the genuine article. In any case, he must have been desperate to approach my battered old boat.

I rolled down my window and handed him a dollar bill. He accepted it graciously and our eyes locked for a few seconds. There was something about him. He turned and headed off for the gleaming red Jaguar behind us. He definitely seemed familiar. Throughout the trip to Palm Springs, I kept trying to work out who he was. Then it suddenly came to me. That pan handler had been my dreaded maths teacher at prep school in London nearly thirty years ago.

A few days later, I combed the area where he had approached me in the vain hope that I would encounter Mr Harrington, the mellow teacher from Putney who had ended up as a gentleman of the road in Los Angeles. But I never saw him again.

The drive out to the desert community of Palm Springs takes about two hours from Los Angeles. More than half of the journey is spent on the racetrack freeways that forge a path through the centre of La La Land. The 405 is a five lane stretch of tarmac that has an average of 500 cars on each half mile of freeway at any given time of day, travelling at average speeds of less than 20mph at peak time.

The bottom line about driving on the 405 seems to be that you weave in and out of the fast and slow lanes whenever you spot a gap. It's totally illegal to overtake on the inside lanes, but everyone does it. I've never seen a police cruiser pull up a motorist for this offence. But you have to keep a constant eye out on both sides of your vehicle. After some months, and a number of near misses that could have reduced my boat to a piece of twisted metal, I decided to keep my rear tailgate window open the entire time I was on the freeway. It meant that I could hear vehicles behind me even if they were hidden by the blind spot in my rear view mirrors. In the U.S. many station wagons have windows that wind down at the back, so my tip is to keep them open. It's never that cold in La La Land – and it might help save your life.

Once we had negotiated the 405, we switched to the 10, which is a picnic in comparison. But here we were driving through areas that make turning off the freeway a very ill-advised manoeuvre. Some of these districts are very dangerous. Let them flash past you at 65mph but don't stop for a bar of chocolate or you may end up being the umpteenth victim of a gang shoot-out that day.

The scenery on all LA freeways is pretty much the same – lots of gaudy billboards, flashing neon lights proclaiming incredible new car bargains, 100 foot high signs warning motorists they are just approaching a *Denny's Restaurant* or a *Wendy's*.

Having finally exited the grand metropolis we soon found ourselves on a fairly quiet strip of freeway blacktop on the edge of the desert. Hundreds and hundreds of propellor-like objects on flag poles came into view. The light desert winds were turning them around like futuristic windmills. They seemed familiar.

"Thelma and Louise!"

"What?" said my wife.

"They drove through them when the police were chasing them."

My arrival in La La Land was complete. Real life had just been taken over by movie memory. We were here to stay.

These strange mechanical devices actually help supply the entire Palm Springs area with electricity.

As we turned onto Highway 111 towards the city of Palm Springs, the Santa Rosa mountains emerged to our right and Mount San Jacinto away to the left. The overlooking peaks were so high they blocked out the sun from the town as early as 3 o-clock on that hot November afternoon.

Palm Springs has turned from an oasis into a thriving city, thanks to the Agua Caliente Indians' ancient miracle healing waters which still flow beneath the city streets. These springs were said to have magical powers and aided thousands of sick and needy people. They also first attracted American entrepreneurs to the area who ultimately turned this town into what it is today.

Palm Springs' main street is called Palm Canyon Drive and it seems to stretch for miles and miles with a vast array of stores, supermarkets, antique shops and the occasional motel that tends to include the words "sun" and/or "palms" in its title.

We stopped to stretch our legs and take a look around. The journey had taken about the same time as it would to go west on the M40 from London to Oxford, but we had covered almost twice that distance. We enjoyed a tasty cappuccino in a friendly diner called *Joe's*, to be recommended, before beginning the search for a hotel.

I remembered my producer friend from Paramount assuring me: "It'll be empty this time of year. Season doesn't get goin' until December." Fifteen full hotels later and I made a mental note never to return one of his calls again.

We were working inwards towards the centre of Palm Springs again by the time darkness fell. Then Clare spotted a brass plaque on a set of discrete double doors in a quiet residential street just off the main drag.

A bronzed-looking character in a pair of green Bermudas and a T-shirt opened the door and thankfully welcomed us in.

Our new best friend turned out to be an Englishman named Peter, owner of the Raffles Hotel. Peter was delighted to be greeting two compatriots. Within minutes, we knew everything there was to know about Peter's childhood in London, his career as a window dresser at Robinsons, on Oxford Street and about his partner, Barry.

Raffles isn't exactly your usual motel. A vast mural makes a backdrop for the Roman baths-shaped swimming pool, hundreds of wooden parrots perch from the walls, and there are wicker chairs under the porches of the 12 separate cabins. We seemed to have stumbled upon a "little piece of paradise in the middle of the desert," as Peter described it.

Peter revealed that before he purchased it, the property had been a rather rundown version of Alfred Hitchcock's Bates Motel.

That evening we took a stroll down Palm Canyon Drive and ended up in one of those traditional American restaurants you would expect to find in the centre of New York, rather than the desert community of Palm Springs.

Sorrentino's was so crowded that if it had been on stilts it probably would have toppled over from the sheer weight of the customers. The food was good, but relatively expensive – $50 for one course each for two of us, including just one glass of wine. I think I would have been more satisfied at the fast food joint down the street.

Next morning, we discovered another unusual thing about Raffles. We emerged for breakfast only to stop dead in our tracks. Everybody was lying by the side of the pool – stark naked!

We stared as a plump woman wearing little other than her shoulder length auburn hair emerged from the pool.

This "little piece of paradise in the middle of the desert" is a mini-naturalist colony that spends much of its funds advertising for guests in *Health and Efficiency* magazine.

Just then, Peter – thankfully still fully-clothed – floated by casually and said: "We're a clothing optional hotel. But don't feel under any pressure to strip off for goodness sakes."

"Doesn't it feel great to just be able to walk naked without anyone hassling you, man?" asked the well-endowed hunk eating the complimentary 'Australian' breakfast next to us.

Eyes averted, I nodded my head and then noticed Clare inspecting him. I decided we should check out of Raffles before she made too many comparisons.

Before leaving Palm Springs, we took up one of Peter's recommendations for lunch. *Le Vallauris*, on Tahquitz Canyon Way, nestles picturesquely at the foot of the mountains that overlook the town. It prides itself on providing the freshest food in Palm Springs. The cuisine is mainly French, but their are also hints of Italian and South Pacific food on the menu.

We had Lake Superior whitefish on a bed of leaf spinach with a Dijon mustard mouseline. The chef prides himself on his black ravioli with lobster and tomato oil and I was also tempted by the roasted rack of lamb with raspberry sauce.

Le Vallauris is worth a repeat visit some day.

There are an estimated 700 cult groups in California with more than a million members and a range of philosophies that is mind boggling. It seems that the majority of followers are attracted by the charisma of a leader or the warmth and enthusiasm of a cult's members.

In mid-November I succumbed to one such religious fanatic in a desperate attempt to cure my ailing back.

His name was Doctor Khalsa and he belonged to one of La La Land's vast number of cults and religious sects. He also happened to be the only person in Los Angeles capable of curing my painful back problems.

I stumbled upon Dr Khalsa at his swish offices on one of the Cedar's Sinai tower blocks after being rejected for treatment by thirty other so-called back experts. They had all refused to do the corrective treatment essential to solve my back injury because they were afraid that if something went wrong I might sue them.

Suing is big business in California. People will sue for anything from tripping on sidewalks to sustaining injuries while breaking into someone else's home! Lawyers claim that this obsession with litigation has led to safer places and practises. But the down side is that whole towns have gone bankrupt and schools have lost their playgrounds because they can't afford insurance cover. Some churches won't even house the homeless any longer because they lack sufficient cover.

But Dr Khalsa wasn't worried about all this. His Sikh beliefs did not include the La La Land paranoia about being sued. When I first encountered him, he told me all about how he had given up anger, rage, hypocrisy and intolerance, then twisted my arm so severely that I screamed out in agony. Indian music piped through his surgery and a water fountain bubbled therapeutically as Dr Khalsa, complete with turban and orange robes, jerked my thigh across my body in an effort to click my back into place.

The doctor had become a member of the Sikh Dharma of the Western Hemisphere after graduating from college in

San Diego ten years earlier. His name had then been Ray Shelton, from Hermosa Beach, and his father was a high school teacher.

"I was a lost soul. It was a chance to just give up all my worries and frustrations," he explained to me.

My only concern that afternoon was the enthusiasm Dr Khalsa was showing for my ailing back. He leaned across me so that the pungent smell of his last garlic enhanced vegetarian meal wafted from his flowing rusty beard into my face. He told me he had given up meat, fish, eggs and "all intoxicants".

At that moment, he performed a savage manoeuvre with my left leg. A few minutes later I emerged from his surgery completely recovered and singing the praises of Sikhs and alternative medicine.

Towards the end of November, an American friend called up and asked me what we were doing for Thanksgiving.

"Thanksgiving? Is it a public holiday?" I asked him innocently.

"Sure it is buddy. You're supposed to ask your relatives and friends over for a big turkey lunch."

"But that's what we do on Christmas Day surely?"

"Forget Christmas buddy. This is Los Angeles."

Thursday, November 28th was the big day. Basically, Thanksgiving seems to be an excuse for the turkey breeders of the USA to triple their income overnight. It is held on the fourth Thursday of November to commemorate a supposed feast between the Indians and the Pilgrims in 1621. If it had not been for the Indians befriending the Pilgrims during that winter, the Pilgrims would have starved. And now Americans reserve a national holiday each year and eat turkey and pumpkin pie.

At first, we decided to be very British and boring and not even attempt to celebrate. Then, as more and more friends called up to ask us what we were going to do on Thanksgiving, I realised that what they were really saying was: "You've got so many kids we couldn't possibly have you over to our house, but we'd love to come to you."

Eventually, we caved in and decided to go the whole hog. After all, if you can't beat 'em, join 'em!

Our guests were two British couples, one Australian pair, two Americans, their French relative from Paris and her friend.

Everyone seemed relaxed and in the party spirit, although there were some underlying tensions between the American couple and the friend their French relative had brought along.

This woman was called Sybille and she did seem a little distant. She was in her early thirties and wore extremely heavy make-up, considering this was supposed to be a relaxed holiday event. Most of the men were rather taken by the fact she was wearing sheer black stockings with a very short mini-skirt.

Trader Joe's best red vino was going down very nicely at this stage and Thanksgiving seemed to be turning into a pleasant, boozy day much in the tradition of a good hearty Sunday lunch back in Britain. It was even warm enough for the kids to take a dip in the pool.

As everyone stuffed down huge mouthfuls of turkey, complete with chesnut and pork stuffing, I found myself asking Sybille what she did back in Paris.

"I work in a club," she replied rather curtly. She did not seem to want to expand on her career, so I did not probe further. I noticed her companion giving Sybille a tense glance. But I thought nothing of it at the time.

A few minutes later, I found myself in the kitchen struggling to open yet another bottle of wine when Sybille tottered in on her black stilettos.

"I'll do that if you like." She took the bottle from my

hand and expertly opened it in one movement. Her hands were rough, with thick, stubby fingers.

She smiled at me, revealing a full set of yellowing teeth. She was clearly a two packs of Gauloises-a-day woman, I thought as she walked out of the kitchen.

Suddenly, Polly who has been going on 21 since the age of three, burst into the kitchen.

"Daddy. Daddy. I want to show you something."

She inched open the kitchen door and made me peer at my lunch guest.

"Daddy. Sybille is a boy."

I said nothing for a few seconds and stared.

"Don't be ridiculous."

"She is. I'm certain. I've been watching her all the time and she's definitely a man."

I looked at Sybille's rather muscular legs crossed at the end of the dining room table and it all began to fall into place.

Our Sybille was a transvestite.

I decided not to say a thing to anyone and instead amused myself watching one of the male guests flirting with Sybille. No way was I going to tell him 'her' little secret. In any case, I think it made 'her' day...

A few weeks later, our American friends told us that 'Sybille' was a former butcher from Nancy called Pierre. They were most disappointed that we had already worked out 'her' little secret.

Another rather daunting brunette came into my life briefly and painfully at the end of November. Clare and I were invited to a recording of TV star Roseanne's sitcom which has been consistently top of the U.S. TV ratings for the past few seasons.

Being in the audience provided a unique insight into the other side of TV programming. Roseanne and her husband Tom Arnold are said to be two of the most powerful entertainers in tinseltown.

Before even getting into the NBC studio in the San Fernando Valley both of us had to endure a body search that was as vigorous as the one I got when visiting the Californian Correctional Facility in Chowchilla.

My host – a well known producer – explained that Rosie and Tom were paranoid about the tabloids trying to sneak reporters into recordings of their show.

"And what they say goes," he muttered.

This was the first clue to the power wielded by this couple. The next came seconds later when I was introduced to a stocky excitable character who turned out to be the famous Tom. He couldn't stop twitching and his attention span lasted approximately thirty seconds.

Before I had a chance to exchange pleasantries, he was bellowing to his beloved wife who was standing on the brightly lit set going through rehearsals.

"Honey. We love you!!"

Tom gazed adoringly at her and then turned to the live audience of 120 mainly housewives and teenagers.

"Isn't she great?"

If anyone disagreed with Tom they certainly did not make themselves heard at that moment.

Tom acts as his wife's adviser, acting coach and cheer leader amongst other things. When she went through a scene that got a lot of laughs from the audience, she turned to Tom and asked him in all seriousness,

"Were they laughing at me or with me Tom?"

"They loved ya honey."

Between sets, Tom conducted a bizarre one-man show and even invited the audience to ask him "any question. However personal."

"Are you and Rosie planning kids?"

"We sure are. Rosie's had her tubes unblocked and we're

rarin' to go. Every night I jump in beside her and..."

Tom then tried to simulate sex. Two minutes later, after another obscure request, he bared his chest proudly to show off his life-like tattoo of Roseanne's round face that adornes his plump torso opposite a vast Star of David.

Roseanne and Tom had to cut short their traditional ten minute departure ceremony at the end of the show because it was her 15-year-old son's Bar Mitzvah and she had just given him a $20,000 jeep.

On the way home that evening, I was reminded it was almost time to buy presents for my own kids. Christmas lights had already appeared in some streets in Beverly Hills and Brentwood. A Father Christmas was slung across the junction of Wilshire and Santa Monica Boulevards. It was a strange sight in seventy five degrees of heat – and we hadn't even celebrated the first day of the December.

DECEMBER

LA women are very strange.
Each one thinks she is a movie star.
Taxi driver Soung Lee

"Phone calls are probably the greatest thermometer of one's current status in Hollywood," says movie director Martha Coolidge.

The 60,000 people employed by the film industry in La La Land use the phone as their most lethal weapon. More Hollywood deals are made via phone lines than any other way and more careers are made or broken. The result is a society where the phone call has become a virtual art form.

"Many people prioritize calls the way the military do during medical emergencies," one noted writer-director informed me from the pages of the *LA Times* Sunday section.

I became the innocent pawn in one such extraordinary piece of phone artistry after selling my first screenplay idea to the ABC television network. This particular project centred around a true story of a *femme fatale* who persuaded her lover to murder her husband, but was then scorned and dropped in favour of a younger, more attractive female.

The movie was 'green-lighted' by the TV network after former Dallas star Victoria Principal agreed to take the starring role. I was told by the project's producer to be on standby to meet Ms Principal, happily married to plastic surgeon Dr Harry Glassman, who is rumoured to be instrumental in keeping his middle-aged wife looking like the perfect human specimen.

The planned meeting with the actress never took place because she had a cold. Instead, I found myself in the

73

middle of a four-way conference phone call between the producer, my co-writer, Victoria and little old me, as we discussed the intricate details of such things as plot development, character motivation and act breaks.

The phone conference call is a battle of wills. The strongest voice wins each time because you have to talk over other people in order to be heard. After nearly two hours of this I was exhausted and convinced we had achieved absolutely nothing, so I used a little trick I learned as a reporter to bring this time-wasting gathering to a close.

I clicked the phone buttons playfully. This threw the very demure Ms Principal for a while, but she carried on holding court once the clicking stopped. Then I decided to really bash the phone. Whole sentences started to be cut out of the conversation.

"I think this may be a very insecure line. Why don't we continue this call tomorrow," I volunteered, knowing full well that I would out of the town the next day and therefore unavailable for a repeat of the phone call debacle.

"I think you're right. Victoria, we'll call you tomorrow." The producer sounded worried that our high-level talks may have been eavesdropped.

A few days later, the producer rang to tell me how impressed Victoria had been with my decision not to talk on an insecure line.

"She's decided to go ahead. But she'll communicate with us by fax from now on."

I never did actually meet Victoria Principal, but at least she got to star in my TV movie.

The chances of meeting someone who was born and bred in Los Angeles are surprisingly slim. La La Land is like one huge melting pot of people from virtually every state in the land and every country in the world. I can count the number of true Los Angelenos I have met on my fingers. The good thing about all this transiency is that you soon become an expert on dialects. I can now tell a New Yorker from a mid-westerner and a Texan from a New Jersey native. And when it comes to working out what country people come from, even my kids have an ear for the right accent.

The most pleasant accent of all, in my opinion, is Mexican. There is something about the way people from south of the border change "the" to "dur" that is attractive. Take Pedro, the guy who comes and sorts out our swimming pool twice a week.

With his droopy moustache and flop of black hair, he looks more like a character from *Viva Zapata* than a pool maintenance man from Ventura. When I first saw him in our garden a few days after we moved into our rented home in Brentwood, I thought he was a burglar since I had no idea that part of our tenancy agreement included an obligation on the part of our landlady to provide a pool man.

After the initial confusion, we offered Pedro a cup of tea like any Brit would back home. He looked bemused at the offer. Later, he told me that we were the first people he worked for who even acknowledged his existence, let alone provided him with refreshment. Pedro was servicing about fifty pools a week, so that says a lot for the residents of Los Angeles.

People in America are always quizzing me about the British class system. But here in La La Land there is a much more rigidly defined version; money speaks louder than any title. And many of those who have a lot of it, tend to treat the less well off with appalling contempt.

Pedro is a classic example. He had moved with his family from the relatively happy poverty of the streets of Caborca just south of the Mexican border with Arizona, to the dangerous neighbourhoods of south central Los Angeles. His main motive – and that of the millions of other Mexicans who've flooded into California – is work. The average Mexican feels the sort of moral obligation to work that would put many people to shame.

Basically, Pedro and his compatriots seem willing to do any job, just so long as they earn enough to keep their families. This admirable trait can lead to the most outrageous exploitation. If you drive through the richest, swishest streets of Beverly Hills during any weekday, you'll see scruffy pick-ups parked outside multi-million dollar mansions. These are the Mexicans' vehicles – and you can be certain they are working around the clock as gardeners, maids, nannies, poolmen and all for relatively little money.

I found it uncomfortable to have Pedro come and clean out my pool twice a week. If I'd owned the house I would have done it myself. But our stern landlady insisted. Gradually, he began to open up about his background. I was intrigued. I asked him why he didn't go back to Mexico.

"Oh. I do go back most weekends," he replied matter of factly.

His home town was at least ten hours drive away, not including the two-hour wait at the border crossing. But Pedro happily explained how he drove his pick-up truck about 100,000 miles a year by going backwards and forwards to his native land. It was painfully obvious that he preferred Mexico to La La Land.

"But there are no swimming pools in Caborca," he added with a smile.

In the first week of December, Pedro took me downtown to get a new rear windscreen for the Chevy – the original had been mysteriously smashed when the car was parked outside our house. He assured me it would save me $100 if I went to a very special place he knew of.

He woke me at the crack of dawn one Saturday morning and we drove in my boat along the empty freeways to the scruffy streets of downtown LA. We seemed to drive for hours before he directed me into a narrow entrance that led to an open courtyard which was teeming with noisy, smiling

Latin faces. Everyone was bartering for auto spares in a scene that reminded me of something out of the *Milgrano Beanfield War*.

"Dis is dur place for real bargains my friend," said Pedro, sounding a bit like a husky Anthony Quinn.

I parked the Chevy after narrowly missing three little barefooted children playing on the dusty ground. Somehow, I had been transported from the grim reality of the slums of Los Angeles into a third world scenario. There must have been 150 people in that little courtyard, every one of them Latino. I felt quite at home thanks to my moustache and dark hair.

As we queued patiently at a counter where they were handing out auto spares like candy, there was a constant throb of clapped out V-8 engines as more and more locals turned up for what was obviously a Saturday morning ritual for hundreds of Latinos.

My rear window started off at the princely sum of $300. By the time Pedro had spent five minutes haggling in Spanish we were down to $80. It's good having a friendly poolman.

Weekends in La La Land we often try to inspect the end products of those studio factories in Hollywood. And so it was one Saturday afternoon in December we found ourselves heading *en masse* for the cinema to find something suitable for all the family. I had spent much of that morning trying to persuade my 10-year-old that *Terminator Two – Judgement Day* was perhaps not particularly appropriate for children to watch, but she had been most insistent.

"Everyone in my class has seen it, so why can't I?"

Back in London, I would have dismissed such a claim as pure fabrication, but here in La La Land things seem to be a little different.

The current favourite with the under twelves of the LA

Lycee at that time was apparently *Cape Fear*, a charming story about a psychopathic ex-prisoner out to murder an entire family. Despite mass protestation from the three elder children, we trooped off to the nearby Century City Shopping Mall to see *Beauty and the Beast*.

The film was showing in one of the multi-screen complex's smaller theatres and all six of us managed to occupy an entire row, bar one spare seat. Amid a sea of popcorn and countless packets of candies, we waited for the film to start. The theatre soon filled to capacity, leaving just the empty seat next to my four-year-old Fergus for any latecomers.

Movie previews were flashing subliminally before our eyes when a rather stooping, elderly gentlemen appeared down the aisle, accompanied by three cinema attendants acting as if their job depended on finding this old timer a seat. There was something familiar about this character, I thought, as the attendants spotted the empty seat next to Fergus.

"Hey. We're tryin' to see here. Siddown!" yelled a particularly loud New Yorker sitting immediately behind us.

The old gentleman getting the VIP treatment then turned towards us and I realised it was Charlton Heston – but he bore only a vague resemblance to that bare-chested hero of *Ben Hur*. As the movie megastar tried to sit down on the only seat left in the theatre, Fergus managed to spill the entire contents of his giant-sized bucket of popcorn all over Rosie. A full scale war was about to erupt between my two youngest children, when Charlton chipped in.

"Is this seat free?"

Fergus turned to him indignantly while Rosie took the opportunity to try to slam Fergus' seat into the upright position with Fergus still sitting in it. There was an almighty scream. Oscar winning hero Charlton Heston became an unwilling referee until a can of coke missed his Gucci loafers by centimetres.

As they say in the film business: "Mr Heston beat a hasty retreat."

The initial excitement of setting up home in La La Land had worn off a bit by the time December came around, so it was rather pleasant when an invitation to what sounded like a very glamorous pre-Christmas party turned up in the post one day.

We decided to eat something before arriving at the house in the Hollywood Hills. We had been to parties in the past where there was nothing left other than cheese and a few dried up biscuits by the time we arrived.

A group of six of us plumped for a cheap and cheerful meal at *The Nora Cafe*, on Melrose, near the junction with La Cienega. This is to be highly recommended. It is hardly the sort of place movie moguls would hang out at. It can best be described as a Lebanese canteena serving delicious dishes of shish kebabs, houmous, rice, meat samosas and a whole range of unpronounceable delicacies. My favourite is the Nora combo which costs around $6 and I challenge any-one to actually finish it.

But best of all are the belly dancers, who gyrate casually between tables giving the whole place a decidedly exotic atmosphere.

By the time we struggled in the boat up the Hollywood Hills, we were all in need of a two-mile walk to burn off the delights of *The Nora Cafe*. Which was exactly what we got after failing to park anywhere near the party.

The gathering was being held at a house that belonged to a close friend of the host, who just happened to be away in New York that weekend, so he sadly missed the 250 pairs of feet trampling over his flowerbeds. Actually, it wasn't so much a house as a three-tier mansion built like a wedding cake into the side of the hill, in such a way that you could imagine it collapsing the next time there's a really big earthquake.

The invite had said "come at nine". In LA-speak that means no-one will show up much before 10.30. We Brits – being the ever so punctual types – turned up at 9.15. That was the first of many mistakes that evening. We couldn't leave and come back again later because it was a twenty minute walk back to the car, so we decided to explore the house and take advantage of the non-existent queues at the bar.

Our host was in ebullient form. He explained that he was having the party with the rather sinister, swarthy looking son of probably the most famous movie producer in Hollywood. I later discovered that this particular character is well known in La La Land as a supplier of best quality cocaine and women. Apparently his favourite trick is to cut up lines of cocaine on a glass framed photo of himself, his dad and Ronald Reagan and then snort them to the sounds of the star spangled banner.

The party was filling up with very fragile looking La La Land women sporting ghostly pale complexions, black tassled crushed velvet dresses and Doctor Martin lace up boots. I got talking to one such lady who described herself as vice-president of development at one of the big studios. And what, I asked her boyfriend, do you do?

"I'm a script writer."

"Really."

Could I possibly have something in common with this boyish character in a pork-pie hat? Perhaps he could offer me a few tips, since I was rather new at the screenwriting game.

Five minutes later, I had extracted the real situation from this "writer". This former stockbroker from New York had been trying to complete one script for the past five years and his girlfriend had been supporting him in his endeavours.

Since then I have met at least a dozen identical characters, all in their early thirties, all earning no money and all living off reasonably successful girlfriends.

"And you know what," one actor friend told me. "When they finally complete their script, they sell it for a million and then trade in their loving girlfriends for newer models."

We headed back for a refill of Margueritas at the bar. Only in La La Land can you hire a huge barrel of ready made Margueritas on tap. You can fill a glass in seconds with what amounts to three-quarters Tequila and a quarter assorted fruit juices and mixers.

I was just topping off my pint glass when I noticed a plump old chap in his late fifties sneakily pinching the rather shapely bottom of the girl standing next to him. This girl molester was an Oscar winning film director, who had taken up hundreds of pages of newsprint prattling on about fidelity and family values between directing some of the most controversial movies of the past twenty years.

The girl on the receiving end of his thumb and forefinger wrapped her arms around our cuddly teddy bear of a movie mogul and started nibbling his rather hairy ear lobes. She had to stoop as she was a good five inches taller than him in her magnolia stilettos. Minutes later he grabbed her by the hand and led her off in the direction of the bedrooms. He was probably just showing her the house.

Some time later, the teddy bear director emerged in the garden with a smile as broad as his bank balance and a different shade of girl on his arm. One of the women in our group whispered admiringly: "He's got something hasn't he?"

"Yeah. A huge casting couch," I muttered under my breath.

The party was in full swing. Teeming masses of sculptured silicone mixed with swarthy, greasy looking types in designer suits with tongueless loafers and white socks. In the garden people were packed like sardines right up to the edge of the pool, which had been filled with dry ice to create an unhealthy mist that was drifting into the party crowd making a few precious people cough and splutter. Three or four characters wearing what looked like walkman headsets seemed to be talking to themselves rather eccentrically. Later, I discovered they were security men hired to control the party crowd at a cost of $150 each. Hosting a party in La La Land is obviously a serious and expensive business.

The Margueritas were now going down at a furious rate and everyone in our group had developed a pleasant glow. I was enjoying chatting to an aspiring actress who looked like a younger, scaled down version of Raquel Welch, until Clare interrupted our very serious conversation about breast implants. I said a sad farewell to Raquel and bravely resisted the urge to give her my number so we could continue our meaningful discussions.

"I dread to think where you would have ended up tonight if I hadn't been with you," said Clare. "I am never going to let you go to these sort of parties alone."

A little later, I spotted Clare deep in conversation with a greasepot actor who had been a household name back in Britain, thanks to his uninspiring appearances on our best loved soap opera.

This particular character had made the fatal mistake of moving out to Hollywood to seek greater fame and fortune only to end up a lonely divorcee, whose work consisted of bit parts in slasher movies.

In the garden below me, the bit part slasher began leaning dangerously close to my beloved.

Now I had a particular aversion to this slimy little toad. I had encountered him years previously during my career as a reporter in the gutters of Fleet Street, investigating a story that had millions of housewives across Britain on the boil. Was this soap star heart-throb really having a raging affair with his leading lady? I never got him to tell me the shocking truth because he attempted to have me thrown out of the restaurant by three beefy minder acquaintances of his.

I watched him pulling my beloved on to the dance floor and begin gyrating dangerously close to her. When I saw his hand slide down her back towards areas that only I am allowed to touch, I decided enough was enough. I fought my way through the hoards of dancers and headed straight for them. By the time I got there, neither Clare nor the bit part slasher were anywhere to be seen. I looked around desperately. This was getting serious.

Just then this creep emerged from behind a hedge at the far end of the garden. I was horrified. Where was my beloved? Perhaps he had become one of the monster serial killers he portrayed so unconvincingly? Maybe she was lying ravaged in the middle of the jungle undergrowth?

"Where is she?" I demanded.

He looked at me blankly.

"Who?"

"My wife!"

A sly grin came to his greasy face as he continued in a flat Northern voice, tinged with an irritating dose of Californian valleyspeak.

"You mean that girl I was dancing with."

He looked so smug.

"She's gone t' toilet."

I was just about to start throttling him when I spotted my beloved chatting at the other side of the pool. A few minutes later we decided we'd had enough of the glamorous party scene in La La Land and elected instead to return home to a warm, cosy bed.

Having only just recovered from the overindulgence of Thanksgiving, Christmas was now fast approaching. I soon discovered that in La La Land the festive season has a way of creeping up and overpowering you in a sickly sweet and very corny way.

We were in the second week of December and Christmas decorations were everywhere. The $10 million dollar mansion on Sunset Boulevard, in the middle of Beverly Hills had been transformed into a set from a Bing Crosby movie. Three miniature reindeer complete with stuffed Father Xmas' sat on the roof, along with assorted plastic snowmen, overlooking a vast illuminated nativity scene in the front garden. People apparently travel for miles just to gape at this display of Christmas mania. And it's not the only display by any means. The *LA Times* last year estimated there were at least 10,000 similar private Yuletide garden displays, all decorated just as outrageously.

The first "event" of Christmas time for us was the appearance of Polly and Rosie's carol singing group.

Their first appearance was at the Beverly Hilton Hotel. A rather eccentric, bespectacled teacher, a middle-aged French man with a Jaques Cousteau nose, conducted his pupils in the main lounge bar of the hotel as bemused guests looked on. Rapidly the bar started to empty as the carols reached fever pitch with Jaques leading his choir with a thrusting forefinger.

The next session was in the middle of the Century City shopping mall on Santa Monica Boulevard. Malls have become a part of American culture over the past thirty years. Just about every town, however small, has at least one. They're considered a shopper's paradise because everything is conveniently located in one place. But when thirty giggly girls decide to block the main thoroughfare and burst into a sickly sweet chorus of Mickey Mouse's Disney Yuletide Sonata, they can appear less attractive.

All the other parents beamed with pride as their daughters performed some of the most corny songs imaginable. Rosie looked just as embarrassed as I felt. But this was Hollywood. One little starlet inevitably tried to take centre stage to steal the show from the other children. This miniature Carol Channing was only ten years old but her sleek, designer orientated *mom* had her in high heels, figure hugging clothes and more make-up than Zsa Zsa Gabor.

When they began to sing a medley of Donald Duck's favourite tunes, the gathering threatened to sink to new depths. But just then a familiar-looking woman with a particularly strong voice joined in.

Oscar nominated multi-millionairess Hollywood megastar Whoopi Goldberg was screeching along with Disney's Greatest Hits! Whoopi's enthusiasm rubbed off on at least fifty shoppers who began singing along merrily. It was the sort of scene that brings tears to your eyes, rather like a James Stewart movie from the early fifties. Little did I know that Whoopi Goldberg had just finished working on a film in which she played a singing nun!

"D'you know anyone who could carry out a lie detector test tonight?"

To most people this might seem a rather bizarre request, but in the few months since arriving in La La Land, I had become the unofficial "local" expert to a number of old journalistic colleagues back in Britain. They had a rather irritating habit of calling me up in the middle of the night to ask odd questions, but at least they always made sure I was paid for my answers.

On this occasion, a certain magazine had obtained the full, juicy story of some celebrity's wild and wacky sex life, but they were rather worried that the Hollywod starlet supplying the details might be making the whole thing up.

I rubbed my eyes and looked at the bedside clock. It was only 4am. But the voice at the other end of the line was most insistent.

"We need one within the next few hours. D'you know any polygraphers?"

Like the true professional I am, I gave them the only reply they wanted to hear.

"I know a chap in the Valley. Leave it with me. I'll get back to you."

I was lying through my teeth naturally. Back in my days as a rookie reporter on the *Wimbledon News*, in the mid-1970s, I had got my first break with a national newspaper when a Fleet Street editor rang and asked me if I knew anyone who could "knock up a poison umbrella". He was following up the incredible story of the Bulgarian allegedly shot with a poison brolly on Waterloo Bridge.

Without thinking about the consequences, I replied that I did. Then I reached for the good old *Yellow Pages* and found a gentleman called Stein, from Bow, in East London, who had been making umbrellas for forty years...

Back in La La Land, I did precisely the same thing and reached for the *Yellow Pages*. There were at least a dozen names under the section headed 'Polygraphers'. Half an hour later I had earned $500 and initiated what was to be a lasting friendship with a friendly Italian American polygrapher named Joe Paolella.

Joe was actually a private eye – or security consultant, as he preferred to call himself. He had taken the polygraphers' examination to qualify as a lie detector tester and now it accounted for more than fifty per cent of his earnings.

Most self-respecting businesses in this city now insist on giving prospective employees a polygraph test to make sure they are not thieves, drug addicts or drunks. The last bastion that has so far repelled such testing is the movie industry – but then around 90% of employees would undoubtably fail on at least two counts if tested.

As a favour to my journalistic colleague back in London, I agreed to meet up with Joe to make sure the polygraph-ing of the starlet went smoothly.

Joe had devised half a dozen questions to put to her once the apparatus was in place.

1 *Did you first meet movie star John Smith in McDonald's on Wilshire Boulevard?*

2 *Did he offer to buy you a Big Mac?*

3 *Did you agree to go back to his house?*

4 *Was his home in West Hollywood?*

5 *Did he try to kiss you in the car on the way to his home?*

6 *Did you have sex with John Smith that night?*

The idea is that the questions should build up subtly to the most significant point of all, so that the subject is relaxed sufficiently to sail through the polygraph without helter skelter blood pressure problems that might indicate she is lying.

Naturally, our starlet passed the test and the magazine back in London gave me a bonus for saving them at such short notice.

Afterwards, Joe and I went for a drink in *J. Sloans*, a rather spendid tavern on Melrose that looks and feels like a real bar and has a ridiculously cheap happy hour. I proposed a toast:

"To the *Yellow Pages*. Long may they exist."

Christmas was fast approaching and it was time to go exploring. There were dozens of interesting places beckoning, but the Grand Canyon was one place we were desperate to see.

Most people probably don't realise that this truly awesome wonder of the world is just a day's car ride from La La Land. We could have flown, but with combined airfares at $1,000 as opposed to $100 worth of gas, there really was no contest.

The drive to Grand Canyon proved a great opener to the vacation. Once we had left Los Angeles county, the freeway became empty and overshadowed by vast mountain ranges. Reaching the California-Arizona border, the ground became flatter again and fine, powdery snow swirled over the surface of the highway. White fields stretched for miles around, dotted with frost covered trees and the odd solitary windmill. We stopped to watch a red-tailed hawk circle and plummet towards the earth before snatching up its unsuspecting prey with sharp claws.

Eight hours after setting off from LA, we finally made it to the Grand Canyon Village, on the edge of one of the most famous natural wonders in the world.

The village itself is just a collection of hotels and motels and a few shops. A modest covering of snow gave it a faintly picture postcard appeal. As we snuggled up in our beds at the Holiday Inn only the freezing temperatures outside made us aware of just how far we had travelled.

Next morning, a short drive took us through shallow forest to the edge of the first corner of the canyon. The children gasped. I looked in awe. Just thirty feet from the road was the Grand Canyon, 277 miles long and two billion years in the making.

Three red helicopters hovered through the brilliant blue skies a mile or so down the canyon. From where we stood, they looked like toys. You can take them from Grand Canyon Village where one end of the main street consists of a bizarre helicopter parking lot.

The next two days were spent taking horse rides around the perimeter of the canyon, building snowmen on a rolling bit of forest and eating vast hot meals in log cabin restaurants that provided fast, efficient service. We even took a spectacular plane ride over the canyon at sunset. There's also a Grand Canyon Railway and the Indian ruins at nearby Walnut Canyon and Wupatk National Monument are worth seeing.

In the village there's a special IMAX wide screen cinema that shows a remarkably life-like Grand Canyon movie that's not to be missed. The film makes you feel as if you're actually in the canyon. The cameras follow a raft trip through the rapids and then take a star-wars flight along the edge of this incredible place.

On Boxing Day, we headed south for Flagstaff, a little cowboy town that sits at an elevation of 7,000 feet, at the base of the majestic San Francisco Peaks. On the way we drove through Navajo country and saw vast gorges and immense valleys about the size of an entire county back in Britain stretching out before us. Native American communities were dotted around the desolate countryside as the deep, twisting canyons gave way to high mountain meadows.

We stopped for brunch at a place called Cameron. The restaurant was run and owned by members of the local tribe and Indian arts and crafts covered every wall. This is a frontier town still time-locked in the old west. A huge suspension bridge stands disused over a dried out river. You can still imagine the cowboys charging across it on horseback.

Next stop was Las Vegas. For all of us it was our first visit and we couldn't wait. The city consists of dozens of high rise hotels and casinos covering an area about the size of the City of London. It was 6.30 on a Saturday evening when we arrived and the whole place was buzzing with activity.

We found a room at the wonderfully tacky Hotel Tropicano which sits like a monument to this over-the-top fantasy world. Gaudy neon signs flickered incessantly. Advertising hoardings offered everything from drive-in weddings to shotguns. This must be the only place in the world where you get traffic jams of stretch limos and you can see Elvis impersonators on virtually every street corner. The bright lights of Vegas are heaven for some and hell for others.

Across the street from the Tropicano is the vast, bizarrely shaped Excalibur Hotel, complete with medieval jousting and floors of Disney Christmas shows, gift shops and, naturally, thousands of one-armed bandits – otherwise known as slot machines. We dined watching a group of out of work actors on real horses pretending to be members of King Arthur's Round Table. Chewing on baby chickens we booed the Black Knight and cheered on a mysterious character who acted like a member of *Chippendales*. Then it was time for the one-armed bandits.

Every big hotel in Vegas has an entire ground floor devoted to slot machines and various roulette and card tables. The children were determined to gamble away their hard earned pocket money on these "evil" machines that suck you in and spit you out again, penniless, naturally.

I protested, but within minutes of the first bout of severe nagging, I caved in.

"I'm gonna put two dollars on that one." Polly was quivering with excitement.

Just then, a rather stern looking peroxide blonde grand-mother dressed in a bright red swimsuit with flesh coloured tights tapped my shoulder.

"No kids on the gambling floor. It's the law mister."

The children looked disappointed, but they were not going to be beaten that easily. They watched as the glamor-ous granny tottered off in the opposite direction to harrass some pint-sized Japanese tourists.

"She's gone now. Let's go back." Polly seemed to be gambling addicted already.

"But, it's against the law..." I didn't bother going any further. I could tell from the look on their faces that this was going to be yet another example of breakdown of parental discipline.

Within minutes, Clare and I were gambling away our children's pocket money, as the kids darted in and out from behind pillars in case glamorous granny from hell tried to remove them from the premises.

I noticed that an old lady remained on her stool at one

particular machine the entire time we were there. She seemed a sweet old dear, but her look of steely determination each time she yanked down that lever showed gambling fever I hadn't witnessed before. The next morning, I glanced over from the reception area as we checked out and saw that same old lady, dressed in the same clothes, still gambling at the same machine. The American dream can manifest itself in many different guises...

JANUARY

Everybody knows this is nowhere...
Neil Young

Only in La La Land, do people go to New Year's Eve parties with absolutely no intention of leaving any later than 11pm so that they can be back home and safely tucked up in bed, well before the all-important midnight hour.

At our second U.S. gathering of the evening, we came to the conclusion that our admirable attempt at trying to mix with the locals for a night of fun and gaiety had failed miserably. So we headed over to the only British party we knew of, thinking it would involve a reasonable quota of alcohol and some good, old fashioned fun.

By the time midnight in Sherman Oaks had reached its twelfth chime, I unlocked from my neighbour's embrace and made sure that the American trying to get a handle on the quaint old English custom of kissing the person nearest to you on the dot of midnight did likewise. He was holding my wife. There was a marvellous, awkward silence as a dozen or so couples disentangled from each other, apart from one pair who clearly had more than the midnight hour on their minds. The woman's American husband looked on furiously. He was unlikely to attend any more New Year's Eve parties hosted by Brits.

Our hostess was just about to break open a bottle of bourbon to wash down the evening's excesses when our two American friends made a hasty exit. But at least they had stayed long enough to see in the New Year and spark off a fresh round of divorce proceedings.

In La La Land, insecure marriages are two a penny and

the macho man no longer rules the waves. Here marriages can break up for the silliest reasons.

"He used to drink," one woman told me in deadly serious tones when I asked why her third marriage had broken up.

"Really?"

"Yes. I sent him to Alcoholics Anonymous but he still couldn't stop."

"He drank a lot then?"

"He certainly did. Every evening he would insist on having a glass of wine with his dinner..."

Some Americans I speak to are proud of the fact that the divorce rate in the U.S. has tripled in the past thirty years. They say it proves that every couple who stays together is truly happy with each other. Which is all very well, but maybe it could also prove that couples don't try hard enough to make their marriages work?

We weren't the only ones celebrating New Year's Eve that night. The Los Angeles Police Department reported that they had logged at least one thousand calls about shooting incidents on that evening. According to witnesses, gunfire sounded sporadically around midnight as local gang members in south central LA decided to "celebrate" the New Year by firing rounds of ammunition into the air. The worst year on record was back in 1988 when two people were killed and dozens injured by stray bullets.

The nearest I ever got to any stray bullets came after my private eye friend Joe Paolella called me up one day and asked me:

"Wanna come out on a job?"

Joe was always offering to take me out with him, but the idea of long stake-outs in rundown parts of the city was not really that appealing.

But this time, Joe had a truly bizarre assignment and he thought it might be fun if I tagged along. He had been hired by two Russians to find out who had stolen $100,000 from them. But what made it unusual was that both men suspected the other of being the culprit!

Desperate to disprove each other's theories, they had agreed to hire Joe to carry out lie detector tests on both of them in separate rooms. Even world weary Joe admitted it was a strange scenario.

As he put it: "These guys don't trust *anyone*".

I was intrigued by the whole situation, so I gladly accepted Joe's invitation to go with him as his 'assistant'.

As we travelled downtown in Joe's late-eighties American sedan through the heat and traffic of a typical LA rush hour, I noticed the wooden handle of his .44 poking through his jacket, a small reminder of the realities of life on the streets of Los Angeles for a former secret service agent turned private eye.

Joe matter-of-factly revealed to me that these two Russians were doubtlessly members of some sort of smuggling cartel and that was why they were carrying such huge sums of cash.

"They're Russian mafia. I got no doubts 'bout that," he added, as he swung his piece of Detroit iron into the entrance of a scruffy motel just east of downtown.

I was reminded of an *LA Times* story a few months earlier that disclosed how four Russian mafiosa had been gunned to death in a West Hollywood apartment. They had accused each other of stealing their hard earned loot which had been collected in exchange for vast quantities of cannibis produced in Afghanistan.

'Sergei' and 'Leonard' were waiting in the motel reception when we arrived. They eyed me suspiciously until Joe introduced us. Sergei and Leonard stuck out like two sore thumbs. Both were deathly pale and wore cheap metallic brown suits, complete with lapels so wide they could have flown back to Moscow with the assistance of a good breeze.

But it was their shoes that really caught my attention, thick rubber soled black weapons of destruction. It was only later I discovered that Sergei and Leonard were both ex-KGB operatives and those shoes were standard issue from the Kremlin.

Sadly, there was no blue label vodka awaiting our arrival in the interconnecting rooms that the two Russians had taken. In fact, if these two were evidence of the newly acquired free spirit of a democratic Russia then it is no surprise that many former Soviets long for a return to the previous red regime.

Conversation was non-existent. They just looked on anxiously as Joe unlocked his little briefcase and produced the portable lie detector kit, complete with masses of wires and gauges that looked as if they had been picked up from a car dashboard.

I was instructed to take Leonard next door while Joe wired up a very nervous Sergei. For at least ten minutes I sat in that motel room, exchanging not a word with a man who made a habit of carrying $100,000 around in a briefcase most days.

The phone rang. Leonard picked it up with lightning speed and mumbled machine gun style into the receiver. Within seconds the exchange became very heated. I rolled my fingers on the table and tried to look unaware of what was going on, but I wasn't very convincing. Slamming the phone down angrily, Sergei stared at me.

"When do I get to be tested?"

"Just a few minutes."

I started to wonder what the hell I was doing in a seedy motel with two Russian pyschos and a gumshoe. At that moment, Joe's friendly face peered around the intercommunicating doors.

"Alrightee Sergei. It's your go."

"Did he pass?"

"I can't tell you that 'til after your polygraph."

Sergei was looking very tense now. He shoved up his right sleeve as Joe attached the equipment to his arm. Next door, I could hear Leonard gabbling in high speed Russian down the phone. If ever I had a bad feeling about what was going down it was now.

Sergei was sweating profusely. And deodrant was obviously still in short supply in Moscow. Joe rolled off the usual probing questions to ascertain his subject's guilt, or lack of it.

A few minutes later he unhooked the machinery. He looked apprehensive.

"Well. What's the result?"

"I'm sorry. I can't tell you here. I'll officially notify you both in the morning. Nice doing business with you."

Joe and I shot out of that motel room at high speed. I was dying to ask him which one of the Russians had failed the polygraph. But Joe's main priority was getting to his car and getting the hell out of there first.

Half a mile away I couldn't keep quiet a moment longer.

"Come on Joe. Which one did it?"

A broad smile crossed to Joe's face.

"They both fucking failed. Can you believe it?"

Maybe lie detector tests are not that foolproof after all.

They say that Hollywood is filled with children whose parents spend the whole time trying to encourage their offspring to be friends with the richest kids in their class. But Clare and I have never cared since we can hardly be ranked up there with the rich and famous. In fact, we did not realise just how wealthy one of Toby's friends was until we went to pick him up in my dented old Chevy.

The house where 13-year-old Toby had spent the night

'sleeping over' with a school pal loomed like some vast gothic monastery at the end of a long and winding road in the depths of Beverly Hills. A rather gruff voice acknowledged our presence at the speakerphone perched outside the twelve foot high electronic gates that kept out the riff-raff of the real world that might try to invade this extraordinary estate. We felt a little overawed. So this was how the other half lived.

A sturdy middle-aged woman was at the front door of the mansion as we humbly slithered to a halt on the gravel driveway. A polite, yet officious smile switched on and off as we disembarked from our battered boat. For a second she seemed to be examining the vehicle with a look of disdain, but then her gleaming smile was rapidly back in place. After all, we were the parents of one of her children's friends.

"Hello. I am Trudy. Jonathan's nanny."

She held out a hand. We made a few mental readjustments.

It emerged that the parents were at a movie awards ceremony in Aspen, Colorado, and Nanny Trudy was most definitely in charge. I noticed the unmistakable nose of a brand new Rolls Royce Corniche in an open garage across the courtyard. She followed my glance.

"Mr Silverstein gave me it to me as a Christmas present."

Neither Clare nor I knew quite how to reply to this revelation. But I was sure of one thing: our nanny was never going to meet Trudy.

We were invited inside the gothic mansion for a cup of tea while Toby and his friend remained in the private cinema watching a not-yet-released feature film that daddy Silverstein had produced and kindly provided advance copies for close family and friends.

Clare soon had Nanny Trudy confessing all about life as nursemaid to one of the richest families in tinseltown.

"You know last week I had to go to a family therapy

session with the mother, father and both children," she revealed.

"But why?" Clare asked perfectly reasonably. Who on earth would want to reveal all with their nanny in tow?

"There were a number of problems within the family."

"Like what?"

"Well, you may laugh, but the most acute problem concerned who should load the dishwasher."

Nanny Trudy revealed that following an incredibly earnest debate that lasted at least an hour and must have cost hundreds of dollars in consultation fees, all parties present agreed that it would be much less stressful if they... used paper plates!

I was having great difficulty in keeping a straight face, but Nanny Trudy was not finished yet.

"You know, it is so much easier using paper plates. I don't know why we did not think of it before..."

It was time to get the hell outta there before we ended up staying for dinner. I never could stand eating off paper plates.

As we honked our horn and waited for those tall wrought iron gates to let us out of that very strange world, I turned to Clare.

"Aren't you glad we don't have millions?"

She didn't reply. I had a horrible feeling she would gladly have swopped our finest china for a few million dollars in the bank.

"Hola amigo."

Pedro the poolman's cheery greeting had become quite a ritual over the previous few months. But on this particular morning, he looked very under the weather and his breath smelt of nachos, tacos and just about every other Mexican dish known to mankind.

"Long night?" I inquired casually. It was enough to spark

off a ten minute conversation about the under belly of LA night-life, as Pedro sipped gratefully at the coffee provided by Clare.

It transpired he had been out until the early hours at a country and western dance bar in nearby Santa Monica. And, according to Pedro, it was a lot of fun.

"You should go there amigo. The chicas are..."

He looked over at my beloved and realised that the chicas were irrelevant. But his description of the place made it sound irresistably tacky, so we decided to try and organise a group visit to the bar – named *Denim n' Diamonds*.

After leaving the children in the charge of an agency nanny, who comes complete with fingerprints (only in La La Land...), we set off for our night out.

Denim n' Diamonds is a completely different sort of joint altogether. That night, the free entrance fee and the fact there was no queue were definitely encouraging signs. Clubs in LA frequently tend to charge ridiculous amounts to get in and that's after lining up for an hour trying to catch the eye of some beefy bouncer who's only interested in letting in the prettiest babes.

The club consists of a massive bar with two dance floors, three drinks counters and an appealing lack of pretentiousness. And *everyone* has to try their hand at a touch of country n' western style dancing, which is not as easy as it looks.

On the dance floor half the people were amateurs trying their unco-ordinated best like us, while the other half were dedicated C and W enthusiasts who spent four or five days a week practising their routines to perfection. This is America and every activity – however harmless – has to have a competitive edge otherwise it's no fun for the locals.

I was feeling I was getting the hang of things dancing alongside three butch-looking slick-moving cowboys when somebody tapped me on my shoulder. I swung around to find myself facing a six foot tall woman dressed in nothing more than a few bandoliers, a cowboy hat and a pair of fishnet tights complete with fake bumble bees. A badge pinned precariously just above her right breast said "Dance marshall."

"You gotta go over the practise floor misterrr," she drawled.

"You can't be on this dance floor 'til you know how t' do it properly."

I shrank a good few inches in height and shuffled off towards a sign that said "probationers" where a dozen or so clumsy footed couples seemed to knocking each other to bits in the name of country dancing. I was being relegated to the beginners' corner. My humilation was complete.

At least I did not have to dance at the première party for a rap film that Clare and I attended a couple of days later. But then this swish gathering was being held in the local IKEA store.

This Swedish furniture chain has become such a trendy place for La La Landers that I suppose it was inevitable that some public relations executive would decide to organise a Hollywood party at the branch that is located conveniently just a few minutes drive from Disney, Universal and the NBC studios.

In fact, a few months earlier I had spent one Sunday afternoon with Clare and the children browsing through IKEA – known in La La Land as a 'discount home-decor store' – when Polly spotted no less than three Hollywood stars wandering around the immaculately clean shop. First there was Kevin Costner looking at $15 chairs, followed by Farah Fawcett who impressed us by agreeing to sign her autograph on an IKEA photo frame for an awestruck employee and finally Tom Hanks pushing a trolley at high speed through the gardening section.

Back at the rap film première, the fact that this was a low-budget movie party at a low budget store was probably lost on most of the guests. But they all had an opinion on the movie.

"It really hammers its through-line in every scene," said one very serious looking writer wearing trousers a fashionable ten sizes too big for him. (Through-line is Hollywood-speak for the film's theme.)

The dress-code at this gathering was definitely goatee beards for men and crocheted accessories for women. Crowds of party-goers swigged Coors beer and smoked, much to the consternation of preppy young IKEA sales staff complete with "I can help you" badges, anxiously watching for any brush fires in the maple furniture section.

The film's stars included two enormous rap singers who spent much of the evening cruising near the makeshift burger stand between the ironing boards ($27) and the laundry bins ($34). Apparently, somewhere in the vast crowd were megastars like Ice Cube, Ice-T and Iced Cream. An MTV camerman – who called himself "the human dolly-cam" – was irritating everyone by bobbing and weaving through the masses as he lifted, shaked and tilted his camera all at the same time. He wore roller-blade pads to protect his knees whenever he hit the ground for some arty camera angle. At one stage a fight nearly broke out when he dropped to his knees in front of one rap star's hot-panted girlfriend and appeared to be aiming his camera at an awkward angle.

As Clare and I departed we noticed one would-be guest in the middle of a heated argument with the doorman because he was wearing running shoes. Is there any male in the rap music industry who doesn't wear running shoes?

My next important mission in La La Land was to encourage

my children to get a hobby. One friend recommended that good old British game – soccer.

"Your kids would love it. Come down and watch a game."

My pal was most insistent, so that was how I came to be standing on the touchline at a game of soccer in Pacific Palisades, with both my daughters, who were being asked to consider joining a Saturday side.

Soccer has grown into something of a national pastime in America – for little girls. Back in the early seventies, dozens of worn out stars from the British football league were lured across the Atlantic to join teams for a national soccer league. But it failed miserably even to cause a dent in the popularity of American football and faded out ten years later.

However, in its place a national movement of soccer for girls has steadily grown. Soccer is now played in thousands of schools across the country – and the U.S. is even entering a girls' team in the next Olympics.

Most significantly of all, I had recently read in the *LA Times* of a multi-million dollar lawsuit brought by the angry parents of a little girl who was kicked by an opposing team member during a local league game. That meant soccer had finally become an acceptable game in La La Land.

At the touchline in the Palisades, Polly and Rosie watched half-heartedly as the two girls' teams slid back and forth across the dusty pitch that was overshadowed by vast palm trees and looked out across the Pacific Ocean just a few hundred yards away. At least it made a change from the last time I went to a kids' soccer game, played on the muddy turf of Wormwood Scrubs, west London.

"Get the hell over! Watch out referee – that was a foul!"

A group of keen-as-mustard parents were yelling encouragement from the touchline on the other side of the pitch.

One particular father seemed very noisy and his voice had a familiar, raspy tone to it.

103

"PUNCH HER OUT! PUNCH HER OUT!"

On the pitch, two angelic-looking schoolgirls were having a minor scrap while their parents were about to come to serious blows on the touchline.

Parents in La La Land don't mince their words when it comes to sporting activities. The competitive spirit is all.

"Hey! Buster! Your kid's a psycho!"

I couldn't believe what I was hearing. The raspy voiced guy stepped in to act as referee in a desperate attempt to keep apart the warring parents of the girls slugging it out on the pitch.

Rod Stewart might be rich and famous, but here he was on the touchline of a friendly game of kids' soccer, behaving as if his whole life depended on it.

To his credit, he managed to break up the battling parents before returning to encourage his own little bundle of energy in her efforts on the soccer pitch. Just then a dark green Saab convertible pulled up in the parking lot a few yards away and comedian Chevy Chase emerged. Within minutes he was also showing off his vocal capacities on the touchline. I wanted to ask if he named himself after the street in Beverly Hills called Chevy Chase or whether it was named after him. But my girls were fed up of watching these female pyschopaths trying to kick each other to death, so we retreated quietly.

"We'll stick to netball Daddy," said Polly and Rosie without a backward glance.

I had orginally intended to get Polly a soccer kit for her birthday but that trip to the football pitches of Pacific Palisades convinced her that dinner at film star Arnold Schwarzenegger's restaurant would be preferable, so we headed off for Venice.

Within moments of landing at *Schatzi*, on Main Street

in Venice, for what should have been the highlight of Polly's year, the waiter blurted out the customary greeting.

"Hi, my name is Brian and I'm serving you tonight."

The manageress had insisted we book an early table because they were so busy. Naturally, the entire restaurant was empty when we rolled up at 6.30pm. Within minutes, I was escorting the youngest to the loo.

In the gentlemen's lavatories, instead of the traditional piped music, a German voice was spewing out what sounded like passages from *Mein Kampf*. I found it most disconcerting as I stood at the urinal. Just then actor Robert Wagner, one of whose claims to fame was his role as a prisoner of war in the TV series *Colditz* appeared alongside me. That stern German dialogue must have brought back a thousand happy memories for him. Unfortunately, his appearance completely diverted me from the job at hand and I stood uncomfortably at the urinal trying to continue peeing. I gave up in the end, but I hate to think what Mr Wagner thought of me as I smiled in his direction while holding my willie.

"The German lessons were Mr S's own idea. Pretty neat huh?" explained Brian when I found him hovering by our table waiting to take the food and drink order.

I should explain here that *Schatzi* is trying very hard to put itself in the exclusive league of such establishments as *Spago's* Restaurant, renowned for the number of celebrities in attendance every night and the fact that you have to reserve a table six months in advance. *Spago's* proudly boasts that it serves more than 120,000 customers each year and takes in $6 million. But at $100-a-head it is an expensive way to get drunk with a movie star.

Back at Arnie's place, Brian the waiter was in a tizz because Fergus was having a nose bleed while he was trying to take the food order. The sight of blood is something that reduces every self-respecting, AIDS-fearing

Californian to a quivering wreck.

The kids ended up ordering 'new wave pizzas' at some ridiculous price and I decided to stick to less fashionable restaurants for all future birthday celebrations.

Meanwhile the waiter's service became increasingly non-existent. Brian had obviously decided that his tip would be forthcoming, irrelevant of his attitude towards us. We left *Schatzi* determined never to return.

Star-spotting in a crowded shopping mall is not my idea of an enjoyable Saturday afternoon, but I occasionally, if foolishly, allow my tribe to drag me into the Harrods of all malls in La La Land, called the Beverly Center, which is located on La Cienega. This has been the subject of a Woody Allen film *Scenes At The Mall* and its huge red neon sign attracts a cross section of the LA population, Everything is under one roof, four storeys of shops, cinemas and restaurants. And on Saturdays, tinseltown celebrities venture down from their castles in the nearby hills to go shopping with their families. Eddie Murphy and lovechild are regulars and they say Bruce Willis can't resist the place.

At Polly's request, I was looking at some supposedly heart-tugging puppies in the Beverly Center Pet Store one particularly busy Saturday in January.

"Go on Daddy. Hold him."

But I did not really want to bond with a sweet looking baby rottweiler that would no doubt grow up to be a vicious, terrifying brute of an animal. Next, she tried to make me stroke an albino alsatian with long fur. When I was then threatened with a hulking, blue-gray creature called a Neopolitan mastiff that had a face like George Burns, I retreated to the men's clothing store next door. Four kids, a cat, a rabbit and a constant flow of visiting coyotes is quite enough for one family.

I was flicking through a pile of polo shirts when I became

aware of two little girls staring at me. They looked a bit like members of the Jackson Five back when young Michael still had his high-pitched voice. Suddenly they started giggling out loud.

"Hey mister. My sister reckons you're Magnum."

I stared at them blankly.

"Will you sign your autograph for us?"

La La Land had well and truly caught up with me. I was being mistaken for Tom Selleck in the middle of the Beverly Center. What next? I tried to let them down gently.

"Afraid not. He's much older than me."

The girls were looking doubtful when a woman I presumed to be the mother came bounding into the shop. She grabbed my arm and fluttered her eyelids before thrusting a magazine into my hand.

"Please! Just sign it anywhere!"

I tried to protest but this threesome of Magnum fans just wouldn't believe me.

"Come on. Just an autograph then we'll leave you in peace."

In the end I scribbled 'Tom Selleck' on the corner of the magazine and prayed they would not discover I was a fraud.

I was rescued a few seconds later when Polly appeared and tried to drag me back into the pet store to look at a baby St Bernard who probably consumed more steak in a day than the rest of us ate in a month. Only five seconds of Hollywood fame. Oh well . . .

Twenty-six miles across the Pacific lies a very different world from the sprawling metropolis of Los Angeles. Here is a place where violence is virtually non-existent. Where isolation is the ultimate goal. An enclave of old values.

Before dawn one Sunday morning we set off to the port of San Pedro to catch a hydrofoil to Santa Catalina Island

and its capital of Avalon, a town that sets long before the sun each night.

Catalina is geographically LA's equivalent to the Isle of Wight. But it has been carefully under-developed to appear to be stuck in a pleasant time warp. To many, it is a little piece of Europe off the coast of California. This is not the only island in LA County, but it is the most perfect.

For thirty thousand years, aboriginal tribes inhabited the island and when the Spanish came in the 1600s they dubbed the natives as "white skinned Indians". A hundred years ago there was even a Chinese colony on Catalina.

The sunrise cruise across the ocean provided the kids with time to look out for sharks, dolphins and the whales that inhabit these parts. Not to mention the barracuda.

Approaching Catalina, only the peaks of the hills were visible, rising out of an early morning mist. The ship's horn blasted a route through the fog and Avalon, the quaintly named capital of the island, finally appeared through the mist with its narrow streets and pretty little craftsmen's cottages built into the hillside. Avalon has 3,000 residents and almost as many T-shirt shops.

A golden yellow strip of beach separates the town from the ocean and people were already swimming, even though the sun had only just risen. Residents on the streets were strolling rather than rushing to their destinations.

It took just three minutes to wander across town to catch the bus for a trip around the island. This is the only permissible means of transport outside the town because 'non-essential' vehicles are banned from most of the island to help preserve it ecologically. Even in Avalon there are only a handful of cars on the road.

A steep hillside road took us high up above Avalon towards the hilly terrain that makes up most of the 42,000 acres of Catalina. Below, the town became smaller and smaller as the bus slowly wound its way round the blind corners and steep grades of De Scanso Canyon Road.

High above one peak, we saw two eagles flying grace-fully through the air patrolling their territory for intruders. Squirrels and chipmunks scurried up and down almost every tree trunk. A handful of deer nibbled grass near the road.

The terrain flattened out for a few miles and we came across a field of bison, drinking water from a small lake on the edge of a tiny forest. Not even a man-made fence hemmed them in. It could have been a scene from a hun-dred, or even two hundred years ago.

We stopped for a snack at the aptly named *Airport-in-the-Sky* Restaurant, created in 1948 when two mountains were levelled off and a whole canyon filled in to make way for progress. Planes take off literally from the edge of a cliff. If they don't lift off there is only one way to go.

On our return to Avalon, I got talking to a pleasant elderly man called George who said he was once mayor of the town.

"This is just a different world from over there," he said waving his finger vaguely in the direction of the mainland in the distance. The whole island seems to work on the premise that it is different from the rest of the world.

"And it will always be that way," added George deter-minedly.

FEBRUARY

LA is in the business of dreams.
Nathanael West

The first sign that the weather had taken a dramatic turn for the worse came as I opened the curtains to the French doors that overlooked what Americans call the backyard. The wind was sweeping waves of water over the edge of the pool and down onto the rose bushes on the garden bank below. Buckets of rain cascaded from the sky. All this came as a bit of a surprise. This is the place where cars never rust, where houses have wafer thin wooden roofs and sun worshippers can hit the beaches just about all year round.

Concerned local politicians and civil servants tell us that if the city doesn't get a reasonable amount of rain, then all water supplies will be depleted by the year 2000. So no doubt they were delighted when the clouds exploded in February, sending millions of gallons of water onto the streets of La La Land for weeks and weeks in the area's heaviest rainfall for many years.

As the swimming pool overflowed into the needy flower beds, I risked a drenching and ran out to the driveway to grab what I expected to be a soggy daily newspaper. Not in La La Land. Here when it rains the paper comes sealed in a plastic bag. Yet when it's sunny it turns up with just a thin piece of string holding it together. Goodness knows how many poor souls are hired to watch the weather reports each day before deciding whether the paper should come wrapped or fresh.

The paper itself got swept up by flooding mania. Day

111

after day the front page was dominated by stories and pictures about the rain.

"WORST FLOODS IN FIFTY YEARS" screamed the headline that morning. The photograph below showed a man sitting on the roof of his immersed automobile as it was swept along by a torrent of water on what had been a street a few hours earlier. I read the caption and found that this frightening scene had occurred in the Sepulveda Basin, just a few miles north. Ten minutes drive away were scenes of death and destruction. I switched on the TV for the up-date on the situation. The breakfast news shows were giving the mass flooding their unique brand of saturation coverage. The bulk of their footage was taken from the relative safety of helicopters hovering above poor, helpless residents more interested in saving their lives and property than appearing on prime-time news.

The kids were soon up and screaming with excitement at the distinct possibility that the swimming pool might actually end up in the house. As their school was perched on the top of a hill overlooking central Los Angeles, I knew that the heavy rainfall wouldn't affect it. But the journey to school was a bit like driving through Calcutta during the monsoon, only the cars are twice the size and twice as badly driven.

People were skidding across busy junctions, losing control of their vehicles at every corner and braking just as late as they usually did in dry weather, only to discover that anti-lock brakes do just the opposite on rain-drenched roads. At every crossroads, I said a silent prayer and crossed my fingers in the hope that a Stirling Moss of LA would not be trying to jump the lights.

I nearly sliced a man driving a Camaro in half when I went into a skid on a busy stretch of road after completely losing control of the boat for a few seconds. The roads in La La Land get so little rain that the oil from millions of seeping engines combines with the water to turn many of the roads into the equivalent of black ice.

Now I know why you have to stick to the quiet side streets when it rains in LA.

Back at the house, serious leaks in three rooms were spouting through the flimsy wooden roof. It was time to call in a handyman if we were to save the house from becoming an indoor swimming pool.

Tony the handyman turned out to be another piece of London. He was Dublin-born with a marvellous Irish brogue, even though he had lived in the same area of south London as us for many years. What on earth brought him out to the madness of La La Land was beyond me. But then so many weird and wonderful souls turn up in the City of Angels.

Like all the rest of us ex-pats, he drove a vast gas guzzler from the mid-seventies that looked like something Kojak would have used on the streets of New York. We talked about why American automobiles are the best value to buy. We talked about why you can't get Marmite in U.S. supermarkets. We talked about the only good place for a real pint of Guinness in the city. We even talked about how the sidewalks of La La Land are most certainly not paved with gold.

And eventually, Tony got around to fixing the three leaks. It took him most of the day, but he wasn't charging by the hour, so we didn't mind.

Meanwhile, doomwatch predictions from so-called weather experts made it sound as if the whole city was about to be washed away by a huge tidal wave.

We stayed in for most of the three or four days of the worse flooding watching the TV news footage going from excess to hysteria. It was strange to be huddled in front of a blazing fire just a few days after having been happily swimming in the pool.

After it all subsided, I was amused to see vast lines of cars forming at car washes throughout La La Land. One local explained to me that these desperate drivers were so determined to rid their once gleaming autos of every scrap of mud and grime that they were quite prepared to wait for up to three hours at their nearest car wash.

"It's a matter of great importance to them. A clean car means everything to most of these people," he told me.

A few weeks later, the good old *LA Times* revealed that department stores were now selling a special line of men's and women's clothing that included "black jumpsuits complete with car wash panels" so that La La Landers could give their automobiles a quick once over with a chamois cloth at a moment's notice.

According to La La Land folklore, when it rains in the City of Angels, it snows in the surrounding ski-resorts.

That may sound far fetched, but it is absolutely true. So, after a washed-out few weeks in Los Angeles, we took our life in our hands and hit the rain sodden freeway to head for Big Bear, in the San Bernadino mountains.

Less than an hour and a half from Brentwood, we came across our first snow plough and entered a fairy tale white world. Toboganning down 100 foot hills, driving snow-mobiles through the forest and eating huge portions of roast beef at *Arby's* Restaurant turned the weekend into a highly enjoyable 36-hour trip. And all it cost was a night in a cheap motel and $25 in gas. It really is true what they say about La La Land; there's so much to do, there aren't enough days in the year to do it.

The thing about moving your entire family to a completely new country is that you have to make much more effort to find real friends. So in La La Land we went to a number of dinner parties to try to get to know people – warts and all.

Unfortunately, you meet some people and think you know *where they are coming from*, only to be stunned by

114

how wrong you are. On other occasions, you meet people who are basically great fun but spell TROUBLE.

Take the dinner party we were invited to in one of the trendiest areas of West Hollywood. He was a tall, dark, debonair, matinée idol type and she was a talkative little South American woman with an evil laugh and a tendency to wear the most tight-fitting clothes. Their house was just north of the Sunset Strip, a beautiful 1920s Cape-Cod style home.

In this particular area of West Hollywood, many of the houses have been standing for more than seventy years and consequently have real charm, unlike most properties in La La Land which are modern, characterless homes built in the last thirty years. This district is filled with Europeans because Americans feel it's too near the so-called 'front line' between the civilised west side of the city and the sprawling urban terror of the central and eastern districts. As a family who've lived in or near the centre of London for most of our lives, the idea of a few hobos shuffling up Sunset did not seem very scary.

The dinner party was not as we had imagined. Instead of the usual showbiz types, there was a cross section of guests including a lawyer, a doctor, a movie director and a quiet, elf-like character who described himself as a trichologist and hailed originally from Bethnal Green.

As it was a Saturday night, none of the usual LA excuses about not drinking because of work the next day could be made. One vain character did insist he was due in the gym at seven the next morning. We all laughed at him and told him to take the day off. His wife was highly amused by our put-down, as she seemed to suspect he was toning up his muscles to impress his new secretary.

I was sitting next to a New York lady wearing the traditional mid-thirties to mid-forties uniform of tight-fitting black mini-dress with black stockings and black pumps. She

115

was a real giggler with a vast mass of dark, curly hair. On my other side was a more fearsome Californian lady of Rambo proportions and a deadly serious manner.

Initially, the conversation remained low key. Then I overheard my trichologist friend-to-the-stars trying to convince one woman that men's sperm was excellent for the complexion.

"You must be kidding?" replied the shocked lady lawyer.

"No. In fact," his voice lowered, "It's also very good for the scalp."

Just then my bubbly New York friend took a huge gulp of Chianti and broke into everyone else's conversation.

"What d'you all think of phone sex?" she asked loudly.

A wall of silence hit the room.

"It's no big deal y'know!"

My bubbly new friend rapidly elicited confessions from two of the couples that they had indulged in a spot of phone intimacy themselves. The great thing about Californians is that they feel obliged to be open about everything if confronted face on. The entire dinner party changed direction.

"It's the safest form of sex around," my bubbly friend continued. "You can't get AIDS down a phone line can you?"

One droll character couldn't resist butting in, "Give it time."

She carried on undeterred.

"It's such a turn on. My only worry is that it might end up being more exciting than the real thing."

The trichologist seemed in a trance.

She then regalled us with the game rules of phone sex.

"It should be a playful/nasty combo."

Only an American could describe a sexual act in the same way as take-away chicken.

"But what about call waiting? That must take all the edge off it," said another woman.

Good point. In La La Land, the scourge of all phone

calls is the call-waiting system that allows you to put one caller on hold and take another call at the same time.

Another woman turned towards my bubbly new friend: "Don't call us. We'll call you . . ."

The real Los Angeles, rather than the Hollywood glitzy version that exists in most people's minds, interests me enormously. I often stop at seedy-looking coffee shops or diners in some of the rougher areas because I'm interested in what makes this city tick.

I also have the advantage of the Chevy boat. No-one in their right mind is going to bother a guy with four kids in a rundown station wagon.

One day in February I was driving along the dicier end of Sunset Boulevard, (it stretches from one end of the city to the other), after being dragged by the children to a discount toy shop in an area called Silver Lake, which borders on some of the rougher parts of town.

The kids were nagging about being hungry and trying to force me to stop at every food shop we passed. My patience was wearing rather thin but I knew there was no way I would make it back to Brentwood without having to stop to replenish the troops.

Four-year-old Fergus's eyes lit up when he spotted a *Tang's Donut*, just west of Silver Lake, on Sunset. I like stopping in doughnut shops because I dislike doughnuts so much I'm not tempted to stray from my diet.

But this turned out to be no ordinary doughnut place. A group of at least a dozen gang members were milling around the entrance. I felt like turning straight around and heading back to the boat. It's easy to spot gang members; these particular youths had bandanas tied around their heads and were walking with what Tom Wolfe described in *Bonfire Of The Vanities* as a "pimp's roll."

"Come on Daddy."

The children were wonderfully oblivious to my fear. Their only priority was food. The gang members were causing chaos by pushing in front of terrified customers. For some reason – maybe it was because I had all four kids with me – they ignored us completely.

Then, at the far end of the diner, I noticed a table with at least ten men and women including a handful of bandana-wearing customers... playing chess!

Toby – a great chess fan – was aghast at this group of fearsome-looking La La Landers performing one of the most unlikely mating rituals I had ever witnessed, in a greasy, rundown doughnut shop. Goodness knows how they managed to concentrate and what would Bobby Fischer and Boris Spassky have made of this extraordinary scene? On closer inspection, the chess players in *Tang's Donut* were very skilled on the boards. A number of onlookers lazily munched at their doughnuts. I later discovered that the games at *Tang's* were renowned for their fanatical players who often play right through the night in challenge series, refreshed by coffee at 50 to 70 cents a shot. Some of the hard core participants apparently go through at least a dozen coffees in a night of playing.

Nothing surprises me in La La Land any more...

But the bizarre sight of chess-playing desperados munching doughnuts paled into insignificance when I found out what a magazine editor had in store for me later that month.

"I've got a great job for you mate."

The English voice at the other end of the phone line belonged to the features editor of one of the London-based magazines that occasionally commissioned me to write off-the-wall articles. But there was something about the tone of his voice that made me feel a little suspicious. There was an edge to it. I soon found out why.

118

"We'd like you to cover the *Club Fuck Ball*. It sounds like a lot of fun..."

I wondered what on earth he was on about. After the briefest of briefings, I learnt that the Club Fuck Ball was supposed to be the annual get together for La La Land's rubber and leather fanatics and there was an assumption that a number of famous faces would appear suitably attired at this gathering of Los Angeles' top notch pain addicts. I didn't bother pointing out that if they wore their rubber masks then identification might be a little problematic.

"You'll have a great time mate," said the English voice.

It had been a quiet month workwise, so I was in no position to turn down a decent sized pay check. I even managed to entice a good cross section of friends to accompany Clare and I to what was billed as the cross dressers' event of the year. When the tickets turned up in the post, they promised a dress code that should include "latex, leather, corsets, uniforms, high heels, cross dressing and *avant garde* black".

The event was staged in a vast former LA hotel downtown, called the Park Plaza. Our group of ten included a couple of producers and directors, an out-of-work nightclub singer and three very British hooray Henrys with trust funds who were trying (not very hard) to make it in movieland. Three or four hundred colourful creatures proudly arrived, heads held high despite the fact that most of them were dressed in leather thongs or rubber dresses and an impressive selection of earrings which seemed to be piercing everything from their eyebrows to their navels.

But instead of going wild the moment the drugs and drink started circulating, the leather and rubber brigade just stood around the main hall making polite conversation and toasting each other in Perrier. One man, however, seemed to have his hands full with a well-built girl dressed in a rubber bodystocking, complete with thigh covering boots.

119

Then I overheard their conversation:

Man: "I've got to be at work by seven tomorrow. Wow, this Perrier really fills you up quick."

Girl: "If you're leaving before 9.30 maybe I could catch a ride with you?"

The words didn't fit with the outfits. They were dressed as if they were about to enter a sado-masochistic dungeon, yet they were obviously as interested in illicit sex as the Queen Mother.

I began dashing about taking photos of the proceedings, half afraid that some off-duty bank manager would come up and thump me for snapping him dressed in a PVC jockstrap. But it never happened. Most of these enthusiasts were nothing more than faintly exhibitionist about their fondness for anything shiny. Except for Ron the telephone engineer.

I first noticed Ron when he wandered up the main staircase dressed only in a pair of rubber surgical gloves and black leather Y-fronts. He had earrings in his nipples, lips, nose, wrist, forehead... not to mention eight studs in each ear. He homed in on two girls in our party who made the fatal mistake of admiring his earrings.

"Which one," was Ron's pat reply. These girls had just opened up a can of wisecracks from the heavily pierced communications expert. Within minutes Ron was inviting the girls to take a look at the nine examples of prime piercing that existed between his stomach and the tops of his thighs. When they declined, a broad smile came over his rather greasy face and an enormous swelling started to alter the shape of his leather Y-fronts. The girls were giggling as the Y-fronts looked as if they were about to explode at the seams. Suddenly Ron shoved his hand down them and out came the most enormous contraption – but it was not made of flesh and blood.

"Finest invention ever made," said Ron proudly holding up a ten inch long piece of plastic connected by a wire to

120

the side of his Y-fronts. This was obviously his wittiest party trick.

We were saved when a Madonna look-alike transvestite boldly walked up to Ron and starting tweaking at the shark's tooth hanging from his left nipple.

"Wow! Is there any part of your body that isn't pierced?"

Ron was suitably diverted, so we gathered our things and headed for the door.

One thing about Los Angeles that is crystal clear from the first day you set foot in the city, is that this is not a place to retire in. There are very few old people in the west side of La La Land where we live, and frankly, I can hardly blame them.

This city plays host to every race, religion and sexual preference, but it doesn't seem to have time to attend to the old and needy. I was all the more surprised one day when my kids dragged me down to the very lively Melrose Avenue to buy some jeans and I found myself walking past a retirement home, right in the middle of this busy shopping area.

The Golden Age Retirement Hotel sits incongruously in this world famous avenue of the young and restless. It was built long before Melrose took on its trendy reputation, but there is something bizarre about it being there all the same. You cannot help being fascinated by its inhabitants as you walk past. The hotel is like the ultimate goldfish bowl – and the whole world is passing it by.

I was intrigued by all those old faces propped in arm-chairs on the porch, reading newspapers and surveying the tattoo'd, nose-pierced young people passing by in their outrageous clothes. Directly opposite, *Johnny Rocket's* hamburger joint was filled to the brim with young tourists, some of them staring back at those old timers. The message was loud and clear: one day this will happen to you.

Clare and I have already promised each other that whatever happens to us and our children, we will not grow old gracefully in Los Angeles. A house in Dorset or a place in Italy will do just fine. This is a city to take advantage of and then leave before the young faces catch up.

MARCH

I need to temper my aggressiveness with etiquette.
Hollywood producer Brian Grazer.

"D'you see that cop chase last night? Wow that was something."

There were times when Mr Patel, my friendly neighbourhood newsagent, could sound more like a native Californian than a hard working father-of-three from the Punjab. Most of La La Land had probably seen the dramatic car chase broadcast live on all of the major TV news shows the previous night.

It often seems as if the only way Los Angeles news programmes can elicit high ratings is to blast out live action that will glue viewers to their armchairs. However, "live action news" often ends up being nothing more than some petty offence or, even worse, the TV cameras get to the scene two or three days too late. I laughed out loud when one channel announced a "live report from the scene of last Thursday's robbery." The poor old reporter was standing in front of a shut-down shop, repeating the details of a series of "daring" hold-ups that had occurred three days earlier. Why he couldn't have done the piece from the studio or over some old footage of the actual day of the robberies was beyond me. But that's Hollywood, I guess.

The live action my pal Mr Patel was referring to was an outrageous car chase across two states and right into the centre of Los Angeles' confusing freeway system. At least six TV news helicopters had followed the chase from the safety of the skies.

It was very exciting stuff for a few minutes, but there is

123

a limit to how long one wants to watch a Volkswagon Golf being pursued by twelve black and white police cruisers along a very straight stretch of freeway.

But Mr Patel had obviously been transfixed by the whole thing.

"I bet those cops gave that guy hell when they caught him."

"Not the same as back home is it?" I commented as he gave me my change.

It wasn't until I got home that I discovered that police shot dead the get-away driver seconds after he emerged from the stolen car.

A few days later I realised just how normal such incidents are when police got involved in yet another televised car chase. This time the suspect survived, but when he surrendered he immediately confessed to a murder in another state which none of the officers knew anything about. They had been pursuing him for a traffic violation!

Forty-eight storeys above the bumper to bumper traffic on Wilshire Boulevard, Beverly Hills, one of the most powerful producers in Hollywood listened intently to my movie pitch. Above his desk was a sign: "Reality Ends Here."

"Imagine *Basic Instinct* meets *Henry, Portrait of a Serial Killer*."

I couldn't believe what I was saying. Reducing my beloved screenplay to banal comparisons to other films would have seemed sacrilege a few months earlier. But this was the language that tinseltown understood.

The pitch is the writer's sales patter. It is part and parcel of trying to get work in La La Land's movie industry.

Here I was in a Santa Fe pink and green office, complete with a playpen so that Parsley, aged 4, and Love, aged 10, could be wheeled in for 'bonding sessions' with their producer father once a week. The ceramic cacti, the hat rack

124

with horns and the twig shaped pencils seemed to be making more of a statement than the framed photographs of our hero with Eddie Murphy, Robert de Niro and Dan Ackroyd.

Earlier, he had greeted me at his office using a paper towel to open the door and then shaking my hand before immediately scrubbing his hands in the basin in the corner of his office whilst telling me to make myself at home. He was also a twitchy type, swallowing endless vitamins as we talked, taking constant sips of mineral water and jumping up and down to adjust the air-conditioning.

"You need a button," he suddenly said.

I stopped in mid-sentence. A button? He fiddled with a button on his pink shirt. I felt confused.

"It needs an edge," he continued. The phone then buzzed for the fifteenth time in as many minutes. I felt as if I'd just been parachuted into the midst of some chaotic presidential campaign.

"Tom! How are you dude? Can't wait to see *The Firm*."

I waited patiently. This was my big chance after all. He put the phone down. I re-started the sentence.

"WHERE'S MY DENTAL FLOSS!!"

A worn-out looking secretary arrived within seconds.

"Will you cancel my meeting with Bill Murray."

This producer is known in Hollywood as the guy who only likes to make movies with happy endings. He even proudly told me that his childhood idols were Mickey Mouse and Elvis Presley.

"I see movies as cinematic cleansing agents for my own painful experiences," he told me.

I was starting to feel that this particular meeting would have a lousy ending.

"You see, I have all these little tubes in my head. One for each movie..."

Obviously bored with my desperate attempts to complete my pitch, he showed me to the door. My time was up. He shook my hand and then reached for another paper towel.

"It was nice meeting with you. Stay in touch... er..."

He had forgotten my name. As I walked out, a heavy metal type in film school regimental black – jeans, motorcycle boots and leather jacket complete with tribal-design tattoos crawling out from under his sleeves – walked past me into the producer's office.

"Chet, great to see you dude. I think I got you three mill for your next movie..."

Everyone back in Britain is always asking about the famous people we've met in La La Land. But the truth is most of the really big stars are treated like royalty and tend to be just as invisible, with few exceptions.

The nearest we got to one of the best-known actresses in Hollywood was when we visited a friend who was having a garage sale one weekend in the pretty district of Los Feliz. This family was moving to Europe and wanted to try and sell off all their possessions before exchanging LA for the comforts of an apartment in Paris.

When we arrived, the front garden looked like a bomb had hit it. Old pieces of furniture, clothes and toys lay scattered on the grass, picked over by a dozen people wandering amongst the goods. Rosie tried to convince me to buy one roller skate.

"There'll probably be another one in another garage sale some day," said my daughter hopefully.

Polly and Rosie then homed in on a chest full of old clothes.

"Oh Daddy. Can I buy these?"

Polly picked up a pair of scruffy jeans. They came complete with designer rips in the knees that someone called Samantha Fox made famous in London in the mid-eighties and have since been adopted by the cast of *Beverly Hills 90210*.

"Please Daddy. Please.."

My eyes rolled skywards as I wondered how much a pair of used, ripped jeans could possibly cost.

Just then, our garage sale hostess marched up looking worried.

"I can't really sell you those," she announced.

Fair enough, I thought. She's put them out for sale by accident. They were destined for the trash can.

But Polly wasn't going to give up without a fight.

"But they're really nice. Please?"

Our hostess looked embarrassed and she lowered her voice to a whisper as if about to disclose some juicy secret.

"Look. They belong to Julia Roberts. I'm afraid she left them at my house."

My daughter was positively beaming now. An opportunity to buy Julia Roberts' jeans. A multi-millionaire megastar's cast-offs.

I couldn't resist a little joke.

"Don't worry. We'll sell them to one of the tabloids and they can give them away in a contest. I can see the headlines now: Win *Pretty Woman's* tatty jeans in fun competition."

Clare kicked me hard in the shin.

Our hostess's forehead creased with worry. I had obviously over-estimated her sense of humour.

"I don't think I should sell them."

Meanwhile, Polly who had been close to tears during this exchange started to weep most convincingly. Our hostess finally succumbed.

"OK. But there's one condition. I want you to promise you will not sell or try to exploit these jeans."

There are some things in La La Land that are taken very seriously – and Julia Roberts' torn, old jeans are one of them. Visions of a multi-million dollar legal suit by Julia against her old friend for daring to take advantage of her name by selling those jeans at a garage sale were obviously floating through my hostess's mind.

In the end, she agreed to part with them for the princely sum of $10. I was more shocked by the price than by who had owned them. As I pointed out to my daughter on the way home, we could have bought her a clean, untorn pair of jeans for $15 in the local K-Mart. Within a few days, Polly decided to turn Julia Roberts' jeans into shorts and cut the legs off them completely.

"How could you do such a thing?" Clare implored.

"We could have sold those jeans to the *National Enquirer* for a small fortune," I chipped in.

Note to Julia Roberts: *We're only kidding*.

We often meet people in La La Land who either lived near us in London or knew some of the same people back home. The world seems a very small place at times.

Take Robert Lawrence. We had some mutual friends back in Britain and I had also read about his daring exploits as a British Army Captain in the Falklands back in 1982. But I never expected to end up going on a bar crawl with him in La La Land.

Rob Lawrence is a war hero who has turned his back on the British establishment after almost dying from horrendous wounds inflicted on the last day of fighting in that bloody war in the South Atlantic. Awarded the M.C. Rob has 'escaped' to Australia where he has married, had two children and started a new career as a film producer.

A few days after being introduced, Rob disclosed his desire to "take a look" at the notorious *Body Shop* – probably the most famous strip club on Sunset Boulevard.

The former army captain was determined to have a good time. We started the evening with some lethal, mind-blowing cocktails at the *Yamashiro*, a bar and restaurant perched up in the Hollywood Hills with some of the best views of the city and a horizon surrealistically filled with aircraft circling the City of Angels like alien spacecraft.

Moving on to the *Body Shop* seemed a perfectly natural move after that.

A catwalk jutted out into the bar. A sequinned curtain spread across the back of the stage and a handful of men looked on from over the top of their beer bottles.

The *Body Shop* prides itself on being the most respectable strip joint in Hollywood. The manager proudly told me that his club was "much classier" than the seedier places a few miles east on Sunset Strip.

"They're full of coach parties of Japanese businessmen sittin' and sippin' sodas and looking up dancers' pussies," he told me.

The first dancer did a reasonable impersonation of one of the pretty maidens in the "Dance of the Seven Veils."

The rules and regulations of the *Body Shop* state that the dancers cannot take off their bottom halves and they have to keep strategically placed tassles on each breast. Basically, it's no more daring than an average family show in Paris.

The next dancer tottered onto the stage, her face covered by a mannequin mask. Unfortunately, it did not hide the varicose veins. When the mask came off it revealed heavy mascara that failed to disguise a multitude of crab's feet.

We were all about to depart when the seven veils girl from earlier sauntered up to our table wearing a very modest black and white cowhide suit and red tights.

Her name was Cynthia from Rotherham, and she had settled in La La Land seven years earlier and bought a small apartment in West Hollywood. She even revealed the golden rule of topless dancing: "Never run. It looks awful when they jig up and down."

Cynthia had been an exotic dancer with the Bluebells in

Paris, as well as performing at clubs in Tokyo, Italy and Germany.

"You get all sorts here," said Cynthia. "One of the girls is a teacher, another is still at college and another works in real estate."

Cynthia reckoned she earned in the region of $50,000 a year by dancing at the *Body Shop* and at a number of other select clubs in Los Angeles.

"It beats getting a hundred quid a week for stripping at the local club in Rotherham."

Cynthia insisted she was saving most of her hard-earned cash to take back to Britain to start a doll-making business.

"Some of the girls here spend all their money on buying leather dresses by Norma Kamali. I've got different priorities."

Rob asked Cynthia if her friends on a nearby table would like to join us.

Cynthia looked delighted.

"Actually that's my mum and sister over from Yorkshire..."

Following the floods of the previous month, the weather returned to its usual glorious form in March. The kids were swimming every day while the cold winter was marching on back in Britain. Now it was definitely time to explore a new corner of California.

On this occasion, I got my inspiration on where to go from one of the state's most notorious criminals.

Throughout the year, there had been continual reports in the *LA Times* about Betty Broderick, a millionaire's wife who was so distraught when her ex-husband married another women that she cold-bloodedly killed them both. I had avidly read all the details of the Broderick case because I was writing a book about women who murdered their husbands at the time.

It was one of those classic *femme fatale* cases. And it had all occurred in what the papers described as the "most exclusive resort in Southern California," La Jolla (pronounced La Hoya).

La Jolla sounded a civilised place with little or no crime on the streets (other than the odd *femme fatale* case), with vast mansions overlooking the Pacific and a picture postcard appeal.

So one weekend in March, we took the 405 Freeway towards San Diego. Once out of LA County, the route follows the ocean in a picturesque loop. Within an hour and a half, we had passed by numerous pretty coastal resorts like Carlsbad, Oceanside and Del Mar. These towns, which cater for sunworshippers and little else, are nestled just a few hundred yards inland from the Pacific Ocean and seem relaxed and carefree compared with the hustle and bustle of the city.

Another half an hour and we reached La Jolla. The main street of the town feels like something from the Cote D'Azur, with at least half a dozen street restaurants offering a whole range of cuisines. Dazzling white-washed homes tuck neatly into the hillside overlooking the town's beaches.

Just seventy years ago La Jolla had been what is known as a tent city, where farmers let their cattle wander onto the beaches and, according to one elderly resident: "You were up to your ankles in dust during the summer and up to your ankles in mud during the winter."

La Jolla has always prided itself on being separate from the larger nearby city of San Diego. It has a somewhat eccentric image, partly because in this very orderly society, the residents insisted on giving their houses names rather than numbers until very recently. It must have caused havoc at the post office!

At one time, a rather quaint old man became a bit of a local celebrity because he would swim around the bay in front of the town every day smoking a pipe.

But the operative word in today's La Jolla is 'discrete'.

131

There are no neon signs screaming bargains at you. No loud and tasteless colours. No gaudy billboards. In some ways I found myself sympathising with murderess Betty Broderick. She faced the prospect of losing all this because of her husband's love for another woman...

Our first port of call in La Jolla was the beach at Seal Rock, just below the town. Many beaches in California are long, wide and pretty uninteresting. But Seal Rock is a naturally sheltered cove that avoids the ocean's strong currents to provide an ideal children's beach. Friendly seals wallow just out at sea like playful children showing off in front of their young audience.

By early evening, we decided to try and find a hotel. The whole of the U.S. is geared to people who need to stop over at short notice. Standards of cleanliness in hotels are high – even in the cheapest places – and you can be guaranteed an *en suite* bathroom and a TV.

The hotel we stumbled upon was a marvellous family orientated place called La Jolla Cove Motel. Normally, the coastal resorts and big city centres have higher accommodation rates than the rural areas, so I was pleasantly surprised that our rooms cost just $50 each – pretty good value considering the hotel boasted a swimming pool, mini golf, a sauna, plus lots of other activities for kids and a beach just twenty yards from its front door.

Later that evening we dined at *Vic's Fisherman's Grill*, on Fay Avenue, tucked just off La Jolla's main Prospect Street. This is to be recommended, reasonably priced and we all felt pleasantly stuffed by the time we struggled back to the hotel.

But it wasn't to be a pleasant night. For some reason the kids got it into their heads that we were staying at a motel filled with psychopaths.

"Do you think Betty Broderick might come into the motel while we're asleep?" asked Rosie.

In one of the safest towns in all of California my kids ended up nervously spending the night scattered across our bed and on a mattress on the floor. It's a shame we wasted $50 on another suite.

There are 30,000 doctors and 20,000 lawyers in La La Land and you cannot live or breathe in this town without seeking advice from both.

The city's 19 television stations and 88 radio stations are filled with enough medical services to turn any normal human being into a complete hypochrondiac. The most ridiculous commercial I ever heard was as I drove down Santa Monica Boulevard one sunny morning. It ended with the line: "Don't rely on absence of symptoms as a health status indicator."

If you know what that means let me know...

Fortunately, we came to the City of Angels equipped with comprehensive health insurance and I would advise anyone travelling to these parts to make sure they are fully insured.

Many doctors in the west side of the city seem to be based in Beverly Hills. Their waiting rooms are filled with soothing piped music and studious assistants who spend most of their days juggling the appointment book to ensure that they fit in the maximum number of patients. At around $100 mimimum for half an hour, it can add up to a highly profitable profession.

But it's the dreaded word "surgery" that can make or break any normal person's bank balance. Only the other day, the trusted *LA Times* reported how one poor woman had been charged $28,000 for the removal of a bunion! The 'podiatrist' in question thankfully faced fraud charges. This lady's medical insurance – as is often the case – only covered 80% of the total bill.

A week in one of La La Land's 822 hospitals can cost

as much as a year in college. And if you haven't got the cash, then you will be pitilessly transported by stretcher to the nearest state-aided hospital and dumped. LA doctors proudly point out that medical care in Britain is vastly inferior. They point to the fact that British doctors only order half as many X-rays per capita as their American counterparts.

But as a London doctor pointed out to me: "Too many X-rays can expose patients to dangerous levels of radiation. That's one of the main reasons we don't encourage so many X-rays."

Back in La La Land, the medics continue to point out other U.S. – U.K. statistics such as, per capita, Britain performs one-tenth the number of coronary by-passes, has a sixth of the CAT scanners and less than one-fifth as many Intensive Care Unit beds.

We gained a unique insight into U.S. v U.K. hospitalisation when Polly had to have extensive surgery on a broken leg that had not healed properly following an operation in London, just before we departed for La La Land.

She faced identical surgery and after-care at the renowned Cedar's Sinai Hospital in LA as she had at St. Mary's in Paddington, west London, less than a year earlier. The British National Health system may not have the same resources, but we felt it won hands down when it came to the attitude of the nurses, and plain, old fashioned caring.

"Daddy. Why doesn't this bank have bullet proof glass?"

My 12-year-old daughter Polly was, as usual, making a very valid point while we stood patiently in line at a bank in Santa Monica one Friday. Why on earth don't La La Land's banks have even a token protective barrier between their employees and the gun-toting public?

After all, FBI statistics show that Los Angeles is the bank robbery centre of the world. Apparently, there are an average of 50 armed hold-ups *every* day in the so-called City of Angels.

An elderly lady with a sharp ear who was queuing behind us soon provided the answer to this vexing question.

"Oh, banks in these areas believe that personal contact with customers is absolutely essential. I worked in a bank for thirty years and I can tell you, I'd rather have the bullet proof glass any day."

Only a few days earlier I had read a piece in the local paper about a double whammy bank robbery downtown.

Video cameras aiming down from each corner of the bank's ceiling had snapped vivid footage of two banditos holding up the bank at either end and completely separately from each other. Two minutes later, both men strolled calmly out of the bank (through separate exits naturally) and the bank got on with business as if nothing had happened.

As an alternative to bank robbery, the same edition of the *LA Times* carried an article on another way to join the wealthy. It featured a woman who runs classes on how to marry rich people. Apparently in La La Land it's possible to enroll for these lessons in lushing in exchange for just $39.

"Teacher" Brenda Blackman refers to the rich in the same way others describe long-lost tribes in the Peruvian jungle. She reckons she can help money-seeking men and women to "focus their approach" so that they can track down that elusive creature we would all secretly love to meet – the multi-millionaire partner.

Interestingly, there is no mention of love and happiness in Ms Blackman's classes. Instead, she concentrates on what rich people eat, how they live and, most important of all, how to recognise them at a party or in a restaurant so that "contact can be initiated".

She even breaks down the rich into three main categories:

old money, new money and money minions (the ones who are working for the rich and famous). Ms Blackman – a small, hyper lady with a firm bust and a fondness for brightly coloured dresses – is positively brimming with tips for these money-hungry creatures desperate enough to have parted with $39.

Her enlightening information includes the phone numbers of all the best golf clubs, country clubs, tennis camps and professional tennis tournaments. All of which are available in the good old *Yellow Pages*. Ms Blackman also offers helpful advice on how to check out if your partner is as rich as he or she might claim: rifle through their chequebook and study the deposits to 'access' their level of income.

A class consists of 15 men and women and she builds these pupils' enthusiasm into a crescendo of dangerous proportions by getting them to chant "I want to be rich! I deserve to be rich! I was born to be rich!" over and over again.

One spy I know who infiltrated the get-rich-quick sessions told me: "It was similar to attending a meeting of the Hitler youth".

At the end of March, I took out my second-hand tuxedo, dusted it down... and then put it back in my wardrobe. This was not going to be my year at the Oscars. No invitations had been forthcoming. No last minute nomination, or even offer of tickets. But it was gate crasher extraordinaire Bill Hayer's 17th successive year in which he managed to get past air tight security to hobnob with Hollywood stars at the Dorothy Chandler Pavilion.

Bill has perfected the art of gaining access to celebrity-studded bashes and he's even got photographs of himself at recent Oscar ceremonies with no lesser mortals than Jack Nicholson, Barbra Streisand, Tom Hanks and Jane Fonda to prove it.

This 38-year-old Covina resident says the trick lies in persuading security guards that he is an Important Person – one they cannot quite place but should defer to anyway. Bill's secret formula for success is pretty simple: look like you belong. Befriend the people who should turn you away. Exude geniality and complain about the riff raff always trying to sneak in.

"It's all in your attitude. When you feel someone is about to come up to you and ask you what you're doing, you say real loud: Is everything going all right in this area? You haven't let anyone in have you?"

This self-confessed Oscar junkie has spent his entire life on the fringe of Hollywood, where his father was a pension consultant for the Academy of Motion Picture Arts and Sciences. As a boy he used to sneak onto movie lots by pretending to be an extra.

Rather sensibly, he refuses to reveal the exact methods by which he has gained unlawful entry to every Oscar ceremony since 1977, but he did admit: "I know it's wrong to go somewhere without a ticket. I'd gladly pay the $500 per ticket if I were given the chance."

As we sat round a TV set at home watching the Oscars, a huge cheer went up when we spotted Bill Hayer mingling with the stars.

APRIL

LA is a carnival town where there are no concessions.
Wilson Mizner

The whole family went into deep mourning the day Thumper the Albino rabbit died suddenly of natural causes at the beginning of April.

Luckily, Clare was the one who found his tiny, stiffened corpse when she went out into the garden with his daily ration of mixed vegetables. At first we debated about what to do with the body as I wasn't that keen on touching him, let alone burying him.

"There's probably a company in *Yellow Pages* that will take him away to one of those pet cemeteries," I volunteered hopefully.

"What a ridiculous waste of money. You can bury him in the garden."

"It's not that I don't want to do it," I lied. "But..."

The man from the pet cemetery assembled a wind shield around the rabbit hutch as if he were investigating a murder before laying poor Thumper to rest in a little cardboard box.

"I try to be as discrete as possible," he explained to my bemused children and I.

"Would you like the number of a very good pet phychic?"

I waited a moment to see if he was joking. I should have known better. He pressed the card of a lady called Flo Longacre, from Canoga Park, into my head.

"She's wonderful and very sensitive. I can highly recommend her."

We most certainly did not need counselling ourselves, but I knew Flo would make a wonderful article for a maga-

139

zine. So I followed up this lead and met her a few days later.

It turned out that she decided to become a pet psychic after having a vision of Jesus in her living room some years ago. Flo immediately quit her job making beer cans to concentrate on communicating with the dead spirits of household pets.

She says the most distressing part of her job is when she is driving and sees a dead animal alongside the road.

"Those animals beg me to pray for them. It's very hard."

Flo is also very talented at working out what your pet was in a previous life. There is the German Shepherd she claims was once a Doberman Pinscher guarding a Nazi concentration camp, or the white poodle that Flo insists wandered the English countryside as a shaggy sheep dog in the early 1800s.

Flo reckons she can get in touch with the spirit of an animal just by using a polaroid of the pet. I showed her a picture of Thumper and within seconds she was making munching noises.

"I am safe and well and will return," said a very toothy Flo between mouthfuls of imaginary carrot.

"It'll happen some day, amigo. Just a matter of time, I guess."

Pedro the poolman was on his second cup of coffee of the morning and spouting forth his theories on how La La Land would one day be hit by "the big one", the earthquake that locals predict will wipe out most of Southern California.

I had grown very fond of Pedro over the previous eight months, but sometimes he did strike me as a rather pessimistic character. This morning he was smug. Perhaps he reckoned he would be half way to Mexico on one of his regular weekend jaunts "home" when the rest of us were facing death and destruction after 'the big one' had struck.

He had good reason to feel depressed at the thought of an earthquake – they have a habit of emptying swimming pools in a few seconds. Refilling hundreds of pools with millions of gallons of water would be a nightmare.

All this talk of earthquakes provided a blunt reminder that we had moved a third of a way across the globe to a place with more tremors in a year than virtually anywhere else in the Western world. No wonder some of our friends considered us completely mad to even contemplate going to live in La La Land.

Endless inches of newsprint and TV video tape provide a constant warning of the awful catastrophes that will one day come. According to so-called experts, the frequency of quakes in Southern California since 1985 has run higher than in the previous four decades.

In a recently published report entitled *Future Seismic Hazards in Southern California* a specialist scientific panel concluded, rather ominously, that a large scale earthquake will soon occur in the area.

Unfortunately, Brentwood is directly above the notorious San Andreas Fault, and this is the most likely fault line to be affected in the near future.

Yet, despite all these gloomy warnings, the children and I were fascinated by the possibility that an earthquake might occur. They relished the thought of a 'trembler'. They were right to ignore all the pessimism. Life's too short to worry about such things. Leave the neurosis to others. There's enough of it in La La Land.

At school, they are regularly hyped up to a frenzy by something called 'earthquake drill', which involves the equivalent of preparing for air-raids in London during the blitz.

Basically, it goes like this. An alarm sounds and every child in the school is expected to grab his or her specially prepared earthquake pack and dive under the nearest table to avoid all the masonry that would come crashing down within seconds. Any children near the school exits have to rush into the carefully manicured grounds and find a spot completely void of trees or anything else that might be likely to come down on top of them.

My kids report that every earthquake drill ends in complete and utter chaos because for some reason it's difficult to get one thousand excited pupils to behave in an orderly, sensible fashion. Most children sneak off and rip open their earthquake packs and eat all their rations.

These earthquake packs are one of the biggest rip-offs of all time. They can be bought complete in any shopping mall and cost upwards of $30. For what? A few bandages, water, a tin of beans, a handful of cookies, a foil blanket and a torch.

Thoughts of earthquakes and the end of civilisation as we know it were a long way from my mind one evening as I found myself writing a letter to my mother at my desk in Brentwood.

Suddenly, the desk moved without any help from me. Then my computer shifted an inch to the left. The door behind me began creaking. My chair slid back half a foot. I realised I was experiencing my very first earthquake.

The children came rushing into the office, a mixture of fear and excitement on their faces.

"I bet that was a seven on the Richter scale," volunteered Toby.

Within minutes, despite months of being told how to act in an earthquake emergency, we were all sprawled across the bed watching the TV news. Every channel had interrupted its regular programmes to provide live coverage of the "biggest quake to hit California since the San Francisco quake of 1989."

TV news managed to drum up enough drama to fill three episodes of any soap opera in the space of minutes, while camera crews were sent out to interview the scientists from the Californian Earthquake Institute and others headed for the epicenter of the tremor in the middle of the desert sixty miles from Los Angeles.

"First estimates of the size of the quake indicate it was in the region of a seven on the Richter scale," said the newscaster proudly.

"Told you," said Toby equally proudly.

We remained glued to our set until well after midnight watching the earthquake news drama "as it unfolded". Or at least that's what they claimed.

Basically, the TV coverage consisted of three rotating pictures:

1 A very harrassed newscaster unable to cope with the new scripts that were pouring onto his/her desk at the rate of one new sentence every ten seconds. The result was a constant flow of "ums" and "ers" (suicide for a slick La La Land news anchor).

2 Increasingly inane comments "live" from the earth-quake institute's so-called expert, a woman who looked like my old geography teacher holding a three-year-old child with a dribbling nose throughout. Example of dialogue: "Oh it was definitely a big one, I can tell you that."

3 Interviews ("live", naturally) with nameless La La Land residents about what they felt when the "monster quake" struck. Example: "It was kinda scary, I guess..."

My tribe finally fell fast asleep, overdosed on how close we had been to death and fed up of hearing scare monger-ing reports of the bigger aftershock expected "anytime".

"This one could be much stronger," warned my old geography teacher, as I drifted to sleep.

By next day, the TV news had introduced a ticking clock that represented the minutes and hours left before the next big quake, predicted confidently by the experts to strike within 48 hours of the first one. It never came, but it made good television.

The *LA Times* reported that sales of earthquake packs

had tripled since the tremor. Perhaps the whole quake had been stage managed by some crafty entrepreneur, who had a job lot of earthquake packs? Nothing would surprise me in this town.

Throughout the drama, Clare and Polly had been staying at the Cedars Sinai, the famous hospital-to-the-stars, in Beverly Hills. When the earthquake struck the building, it simply rolled forward a few inches. All tall buildings in La La Land are built on rollers, so that they move with the tremor rather than crumble under the stress of the earth's movements.

"It was a bit like being on a double decker bus the size of a tower block," said Clare.

Within a few days, earthquake hysteria faded and we got on with our lives as usual. There were no more concerned calls from Britain. My mother stopped phoning to instruct us to return home immediately. No more outrageously over-the-top predictions of fresh quakes on the TV and no more earthquake drills at the kids' school.

As one real expert said on TV: "You'll know when the really big one strikes. Until then, there's no point in worrying about it."

If I weren't such a bad driver, then I would never have got a chance to attend one of La La Land's more bizarre social gatherings – traffic school.

The Beverly Hills cop who booked me for speeding on Wilshire Boulevard at eight o'clock one morning was no doubt under the impression that a ticket would curtail my habitual speeding. But I couldn't wait to receive my sentence.

When notification came through the post six weeks later, I was positively thrilled at the prospect of attending an eight-hour session at one of LA County's famed 224 traffic schools. The idea behind these establishments is to teach you how to drive more responsibly. The reality is that they have become one of the most popular ways to 'network' in this town.

Locals reckon that since the closure of *Schwab's Drugstore*, where countless stars are said to have been discovered, the city's traffic schools have become key locations for aspiring writers, actors, singers, producers and directors.

So it was I turned up at 8.30 one Saturday morning to serve my eight-hour sentence at the Improv comedy club, on Wilshire Boulevard, in Santa Monica. A bright and breezy character called "Comedian Ant" (he swore that was his real name) greeted me inside the dimly lit club. It soon emerged that he was to be my safe driving teacher for the day.

Ant had been an unhappy flight attendant with TWA until he happened to come across an advert for comics to teach at traffic schools. Using his previously amateur skills as a stand-up comedian, he took the world of LA traffic schools by storm and is now one of the top in his very expert field. Naturally, he now has an agent and is said to be one of the most sought after comics on the Hollywood circuit.

Everyone was very punctual that Saturday morning. It might have had something to do with the fact that they would be fined $100 for turning up late.

We settled into our seats in the club and keenly awaited eight hours of entertainment with a definite message, care of Comedian Ant.

I should point out here that stars from some of the top rating TV shows have been 'discovered' at traffic school. Take Richard Karn as a prime example. He ended up playing one of the leads in a programme called *Home Improvement* after finding himself sitting next to an agent during one punishment session. One star of *LA Law* apparently got her big break after attending traffic school with one of the producers of the show.

This was supposed to be a lecture on how to drive safely, so I tried to concentrate on Comedian Ant's one-man show. It started off slowly with a number of wisecracks. But the tall comic started to get a tad frustrated when his class of criminal drivers failed to respond during one question and answer session on road safety.

"I've got this really gruesome film about car crash victims complete with decapitated bodies and I'll show it right after lunch if you don't all start joining in," warned Ant.

We all laughed nervously. Frankly, it was impossible to tell if he was being serious.

Ant encouraged us all to open our hearts about our sinful driving habits.

"I wanna know when you last broke the law."

Ninety percent of the class made candid confessions.

"I knew I wasn't supposed to make that left, but I did it anyway," said one TV movie director daringly.

"Now I want all of you to share something with the rest of us. Something about yourself that no-one would guess from looking at you."

The class went silent. But not for long. La La Landers love getting things off their chest. The girl next to me definitely had a lot on her mind. She had spent the first hour of the session telling me how she had just quit nannying to become a full-time singer. She was desperate to reveal all and shot her hand up to volunteer for a piece of Ant's therapy.

"Does it matter if it's real personal?"

"Not in the slightest."

"Well, I just slept with my best friend's husband."

The room went quiet. Ant looked awkwardly around. I don't think this was exactly what he had in mind.

Another motoring offender came to her rescue when he quickly broke the wall of silence by volunteering,

"I ran over a cat today."

My neighbour turned to me.

"I guess I goofed up."

The following seven hours consisted of stand-up one liners, more group therapy and some of the sickest jokes

I've heard in a long time.

By the time the full-time bell went at 4.30 I felt grateful for the experience, but equally relieved that I could now escape from the Improv club. Also, my lady neighbour was threatening to sing me her latest masterpiece. I began to wonder if she had actually committed a driving offence or whether she had just turned up in the hope of finding a Svengali.

"Have you got a card?" she asked hopefully. I had to think quickly. If I said "no" then she'd ask me to scribble my number on a piece of paper. Then I remembered . . .

I opened up my wallet and took out one of the many business cards that are flung at you every day of the week in La La Land and gave it to her.

She stroked her well manicured thumb across the card heading and then sighed. "Mmm. So you're in real estate . . . Alan."

The Star Spangled Banner was barely recognisable as the rap artist gave it his own special interpretation in front of 10,000 sports fans. Citizens in other nations pay homage to their country in slightly less extravagant ways than the Americans.

"Americanism means believing America is a special nation chosen by God," reckons U.S. writer Esther Wanning.

That was why sports events like the basketball game Toby and I were attending that evening in late April began with singing the national anthem – during which most people took off their hats and put their hands on their hearts. This is a nation where there are still laws on the books about bringing in the flag after dark, not wearing it, and not trampling upon it.

Toby and I had wanted to go to a basketball game for ages because, thanks to Magic Johnson's AIDS revelations a few months earlier, even I knew what that game was all about.

We had two seats to see the Lakers in a mid-week match against the Portland Trailblazers in what's known as a play-off. This is the equivalent of the FA Cup knock-out soccer competition back in Britain and Toby reckoned it would be a great game to see. At $50 a seat, I just hoped he was going to be right.

The stadium was the Laker's home arena, The Forum, in central LA. Despite the mean streets outside, it was clean and well organised compared with going to a soccer match back in Britain. Every type of fast food was available from carts and stalls dotted around the complex and we even managed to get a parking place only thirty yards from the stadium.

A huge TV screen showed us some of the Laker's recent victories as part of the pre-game warm up. Then these Goliath characters emerged on the immaculately shiny wooden floor and started warming up. Minutes later, the game began with a flurry of scoring from both sides.

The atmosphere was electric with none of those threatening undertones among the spectators that so frequently exist during soccer matches back in England. We cheered our socks off as each side managed to score on average every minute. The game can go from one end of the floor to the other in seconds. There's no boring midfield in basketball.

The last couple of minutes were incredibly exciting as each team swopped the lead over and over again. Players are on a massive bonus if they win and the smell of money no doubt encourages these sportsmen to play hard. We're talking about $50,000 per player per game here.

It was 11.30 at night when the final buzzer went. It had been a great evening of basketball – the Lakers had squeezed through by a slim margin. But the night was only just beginning.

Outside the stadium, we rushed to the Chevy to try and get out of the crowded parking lot before the inevitable traffic jams started forming. Unfortunately, ten thousand other people had the same idea, so it was no surprise when we found ourselves bumper to bumper, just 100 yards from the stadium.

Just then, a black and white police cruiser sped past in the opposite direction, sirens blaring into the night. Seconds later another followed, and another, and another. We counted nineteen police cars in all.

Toby turned on the radio. There was no music on the airwaves. Instead, we heard the same words on every station: "State of emergency." "Riots on the streets." "Fires blazing throughout the city." And then, "The not guilty verdict at the trial of the policemen accused of beating motorist Rodney King has sparked a bloody battle on the streets of central Los Angeles..."

We had stumbled into the middle of the LA riots and were sitting in a traffic jam just half a mile from one of the worst outbreaks of civil unrest in the history of the United States.

I looked over my shoulder and down the street to where those cruisers had been heading. The skyline was ablaze. Thick smoke was billowing up into the midnight sky. Shadowy figures were smashing shop windows. Flames shot out of countless buildings. In the eighties, I had attended the London riots in Tottenham and Brixton as a reporter, but this was on a much larger scale.

I switched on the central locking system and looked over at Toby.

"If anyone comes near the car duck down on the floor."

We seemed to be right in the middle of the riot area but, hopefully, we were not likely to be of interest because there were much more tempting goods on display in this traffic jam from hell. Like the wealthy looking character in a slick suit, driving a convertible Porsche with the top down right next to us. He must have envied us our scruffy old Chevy.

Beads of sweat were pouring down his face. His status symbol of a car would make a perfect target for the hostile crowds that were growing larger by the minute.

The traffic jam only lasted ten more minutes, but it seemed more like ten hours. Thousands of people swept along the streets and cruiser after cruiser screeched towards the inferno that was spreading in our direction.

The radio broadcast appeals for peace and calm, and reports that half the city was under virtual siege.

On the journey back along the freeway, the only evidence of the troubles were clouds of thick, acrid smoke billowing across the blacktop. Every now and again, more fire vehicles and paramedics would rush past in the opposite direction, bravely responding to some of the tens of thousands of emergency calls that flooded the city that night. The death toll was reckoned to be fifty-nine. The estimates of damage to property were in the billions.

When we got home to Brentwood that evening, we were greeted like long lost soldiers who'd been missing in action.

I stayed up that night watching the live TV coverage of the riots. This time, the news shows had a real running story that deserved every bit of coverage it got – unlike the mundane nonsense they usually feature. It was engrossing stuff. Every time I tried to turn off the TV to get some sleep, I found myself witnessing yet another terrifying scene of destruction.

Next morning, as I watched smoke from the thousands of fires still blazing in the centre of the city waft across our swimming pool, there was a sudden deafening noise of rota blades whirling. I looked up and saw five U.S. Army Chinook helicopters hanging 500 feet over my head like huge buzzing insects. Minutes later, I counted thirty more helicopters hovering towards the troubles.

The children were already up and watching the blanket TV coverage. The live news showed people looting everything they could from vandalised shops and restaurants. The anchor announced that all public schools were shut down.

Out on the streets I found the roads clogged bumper to bumper with cars full of frenzied people trying to flee the city like Okies from the dustbowl. Countless numbers of drivers were hooting their horns impatiently as if some magical gap would open up in the traffic if they blasted loudly enough. Being amongst a load of neurotic LA motorists was almost as scary as being caught in the middle of the riot the previous evening. I quickly turned back. The journey home should have taken fifteen minutes, but it took two hours. I have never been so relieved to see everyone's smiling faces in my life. But the siege of the city had only just begun.

TV news reported more deaths, more looting, more fires.

Concerned about friends who lived in more vulnerable parts of La La Land, we offered to play host to anyone who wanted to risk life and limb and hit the road for our house in safe Brentwood. Four people turned up and we all huddled around the television watching as the violence spread closer.

The Dunkirk spirit prevailed in Los Angeles over the three main days of the riot. People stock piled at the supermarkets in a rush of panic buying as if the riots might go on forever. Everyone in the entire county of Los Angeles was under a dusk to dawn curfew. Our food consumption doubled as we sat like couch potatoes glued to the ever increasing violence being televised.

Thirty-six hours after the riots began there started to be signs that the worst of the violence was over. Most of the city streets were empty. The shops had closed down and life had ground to a complete halt. When I ventured down to Mr Patel's newstand, I was delighted to see he was still going strong.

"I open every day of the year," he said proudly. "Fifty people get murdered downtown most summer weekends.

What's the big deal?"

Three days after the riots, I visited downtown. The devastation was overwhelming. Whole blocks of shops had been burned to the ground while a few businesses had been saved from the violence by signs painted across the front windows: "Black Owned." Streets were still smouldering.

As I drove amongst the burnt out blocks, I saw a moving scene, a young mother in rags pushing her baby through the debris-littered streets. She couldn't have been more than eighteen years old. Yet her face looked worn and stressed. I watched as a policeman approached, fearing he might detain her for just being on the streets. But he stopped and chatted and crouched down to gently stroke the baby's cheeks. It was one of those rare occasions when the people of Los Angeles and the authorities of law and order showed genuine kindness towards each other.

Rapidly, a massive clean-up operation began in the worst hit areas of LA. Naturally, a gang of Hollywood stars awkwardly armed with broomsticks led the way. The television coverage remained live, but became as absurd as we were treated to publicity hungry celebrities performing for the prime time news cameras.

Meanwhile, the real residents of La La Land rallied around to try and start to tackle the root of the problem by gradually changing their attitudes to one another. I thought I could detect more kindness in the atmosphere. In the shops, people were being more gracious and less impatient. There were definite efforts to restore some much needed civility. It seems sad that it takes a tragedy to inspire such changes in the city.

MAY

LA is a place where you spend more than you make on things you don't need to impress people you don't like.
Ken Murray

Bears can cause much property damage trying to get to people's food. Park regulations require proper storage of food to prevent bears from getting it. Like humans, a bear walks on the soles of its feet. It can run as fast as a horse for short distances.

A long silenced filled the Chevy station wagon as my ten-year-old daughter Rosie read aloud the huge sign just ahead of us. Then I muttered:

"Sequoia here we come."

I felt like Clark W. Griswald, the character so wonderfully portrayed by Chevy Chase in *National Lampoon's Vacation*, as I tried to reassure the kids that they would not be eaten by bears on our first visit to Sequoia National Park.

With our portatrunk strapped firmly to the roof-rack there was more than a passing resemblance to that classic film which parodies all one's worst nightmares about vacations.

The guide book had promised trees that were "giants grouped in pure temple groves, or arranged in colonnades along the sides of meadows".

That was how explorer John Muir described Sequoia National Park when he first stumbled upon the forest in 1875. Since then tens of millions of visitors have flocked to the forest and on one hot day in May it was our turn to see Sequoia, just five hours drive north east of Los Angeles.

This area is renowned for its beautiful meadows and the

153

statuesque sequoia grove trees, so tall they seem to touch the passing clouds.

Sequoia resembles the most sparsely populated areas of Scotland. But with many of the trees topping the 250 feet mark, it's on a much bigger scale.

Sequoias are the largest living things in the world. Each tree can provide enough wood to build at least 35 houses! Squirrels scurried up the trees at the sound of approaching cars. Clumps of phlox and Indian paintbrush flowers soaked the hilly terrain with violets and pinks. Vast sugar pine trees were dwarfed in comparison with their cousins the sequoias – even though some of them reach 200 feet. Somewhere in the overgrowth, wild bobcats and tawny mountain lions were on the prowl.

The town of Giant Forest consists of a couple of motels plus a restaurant and a shop. Our cabin at the Giant Forest Lodge was good value at just over $100 for two bedrooms and ample space for all of us.

Within a few minutes of checking in, we were headed for one of the many nature trails that make this area a walkers' haven. The Congress Trail starts at the tallest sequoia in the area, named the General Sherman Tree. The tree is big enough to wander inside, along with a passing party of thirty Japanese tourists. As they all snapped away with their sure-shots, flashes of light lit up the inside of the tree trunk. Outside, an Italian couple were having a row about how wide their camera lens should be.

"They must be married," observed my daughter Polly.

The two-mile Congress Trail provided the children with a good insight into the wildlife that still lives in the forest, untouched by human hand. We saw chattering Douglas squirrels, dozens of yellow bellied marmots and many of the 170 different species of birds that live at Sequoia, including a Clark's nutcracker and the dipper, plus a family of wood-peckers busy at work on one huge tree.

But the children still longed to meet the black bear, despite the fact this creature can measure almost six foot in height and weigh at least 500 pounds.

That night in our wooden cabin, I was reduced to sneaking outside in the pitch black and making scratching noises on the door so that the children would believe that a bear was on the prowl in the vicinity. It worked pretty well, until a couple of newly weds accused me of being a peeping Tom after catching me creeping round the back of their cabin next door.

Next day, we found a beautiful spot down by a river bank and paddled through the crystal clear stream as small fish darted in and out of the tiny waterfalls created by the rocks. Suddenly, I heard a rustling noise ahead of us. I could just make out a figure waddling down the hill behind a clump of trees.

"There's a bear!" I shouted. Not one of the children even looked up.

"I promise you, there is a bear over there!"

"Sure Daddy. Just like there was last night," said Rosie.

Just then, Toby also looked up and froze.

"It *is* a bear."

And this particular bear was coming straight towards us. The girls screeched and the poor creature stopped in his tracks and moved off towards a nearby thicket.

That night we sat around a camp fire and listened to a park ranger recalling countless horror stories about bear attacks. The children looked awfully worried every time they heard a noise in the darkness.

But, as the redoubtable Clark W. Griswald would say: "With every new day there is a fresh challenge".

"You always find a better class of pool shark at the Hollywood Athletic Club," promised one of my La La Land friends as we headed down Sunset Boulevard one hot and sticky evening in May.

The HAC is a cavernous former gymnasium-to-the-stars, now filled to bursting point with more than forty Brunswick Gold Crown pool tables.

Having safely negotiated the valets, coat check room attendant, Maitre D' and a robotic twenty stone bouncer, we found ourselves inside this eighty-year-old stone clad building that stands like a testament to some bygone era at the eastern end of the Sunset Strip. Stairs lead down from the private rooms which sport wall tapestries and overstuffed antique sofas where stars like Tom Hanks and the Kennedys have been known to hold a private game of pool. It even has the dubious distinction of being the place where Demi Moore was photographed in a painted bodysuit for the cover of *Vanity Fair*.

The competition on the pool tables that night didn't look too fearsome. A rather forgetable blonde from a TV sitcom, one of television's best loved cops and Eric Clapton made up the celebrity contingent. In the far corner, two girls in rattlesnake boots and Versace black lace were exposing a little too much thigh as they bent over the table for a tricky shot. It must all have been very different when the likes of Errol, Valentino, Clark and Bogie haunted the HAC back in the good old forties and fifties.

Next to us, two cowboy-types wielding custom made cues did not look like the sort of pool players to trifle with. When I accidently nudged one of them with my cue, I thought for a moment I might be heading for the nearest window. But the HAC is all show really. Lots of people flex their muscles in here, but they're all actually disappointingly straight-laced once you get beneath the pierced noses and carefully carved tattoos.

I was beginning to think that the day of the Hustler was well and truly buried when a fellow invited me and my pal to a challenge round. Ten bucks a game sounded a very modest sum.

A posse of five muscle-bound gents led by rap singer Bobby Brown appeared at the top of the stairs. They headed straight for the table next to us and that's when the chaos began. Trying to play a decent game of pool next to a table occupied by five characters as wide as they are tall can be very distracting. I noticed that all five had Bobby Brown's name tattoo'd on their arms. They must be very devoted to one another. But I'm not so sure what Brown's wife Whitney Houston must make of that.

Back on our table, our hustler was making mincemeat of both of us. An hour and $50 later, I anxiously retired to the HAC restaurant, *Drones*, and tried to forgot my losses. In the far corner, Eric Clapton potted the black...

It was May, the sun was shining, the temperature was climbing, so we decided to try and explore some of the beaches that exist just a short hop from our front door. LA County has 74 miles of beaches and 500 lifeguards to prevent all known aquatic disasters, so there is plenty to choose from.

After trying out a few of the typically broad and long beaches that exist in places like Santa Monica and Venice, we realised that a family of six needs something a little more sedate than beaches with roller skating sihks (Venice), contaminated water (Santa Monica) and Kamikazi surf-boarders (Malibu).

So-called surfer beaches are best avoided if you have kids. It can be rather hazardous trying to swim when boards are coming at you from all directions. Surfing is a way of life for thousands of young people out here. When the so-called king of them all, legendary surfing dude Dewey Weber died, he had a boat scatter his ashes on his favourite stretch of water while one thousand surfers paddled their boards alongside and then celebrated with a last ride on the Pacific waves.

A friend suggested Paradise Cove as a good place to go *en famille*. This is a picturesque and narrow strip of beach about six or seven miles north of Santa Monica, well signposted just past Malibu on the Pacific Coast Highway.

You turn down the twisting, turning little lane bordered with lemon trees before reaching a beach that is as pretty as any you could find in the Mediterranean. Poppy-clad cliffs with the occasional multi-million dollar house overlook the beach. Lovers walk arm in arm through the shallow surf.

But the thing that sets Paradise Cove apart from many of the other beaches in the area is its cosiness. It remains relatively quiet the whole year round, a place where families can relax and get away from the hurly burly of the city. One of the other great things about Paradise Cove is that a few minutes walk along its snaking coastline and it becomes virtually deserted. We walked for half-an-hour and only passed a mere handful of people the entire time. Just near the beach is a delightful, family run restaurant that boasts a menu of all the traditional American fare from hamburgers to one of the finest Caesar's salads I've tasted.

As we coasted along the Pacific Coast Highway on the way home that evening, I decided to treat the kids to a slap-up meal. We drove along a two or three mile stretch of the road near an area known as The Colony. This is a bizarre combination of lavish homes facing the ocean, tatty apartment complexes and what seems like dozens of restaurants. Amongst the residents of The Colony are Mel Gibson, Jack Nicholson, Richard Gere, Cher and Barbra Streisand. But no doubt once they are in their swimsuits they look much the same as the rest of us.

We stopped for dinner at a restaurant called the *Reel Inn*. This is to be recommended. It looks a bit like the dark wooden bowels of some 17th century pirate ship. Long refectory tables with benches fill the restaurant, at which you can almost imagine a load of hearty sailors consuming their daily rations in the underbelly of some galleon.

Serving virtually all fish, it's the kind of casual hang-out where movie stars and college students might find themselves side by side ordering their favourite dishes. There is no waiter service in the *Reel Inn*. Instead, customers informally queue up, just like in a school canteen. This is particularly relaxing when you've got kids.

The range of fish available is excellent, from the luscious Pacific Lobster for around $20 to tasty Calamari for just $8. The owners proudly boast they can keep their prices down because they don't employ as many staff as a conventional restaurant. More importantly, they insist that everything on the menu is extra fresh because they buy direct from a nearby fish market.

Towards the end of the month, we were all asked to a birthday party at a friend's rented house half way up one of the many hills that overlook Sunset Boulevard. I had been reluctant to take the kids to this particular event because I knew that the only children there would be the perfect baby/toddler variety. Just the kind of youngsters that my lot would end up accidently drowning in the pool or pushing down a flight of stairs. I feared, not surprisingly in this town, that massive legal suits would follow within days.

Many couples in La La Land tend to have only one child (two at a push) and they pamper and protect them so much that they occasionally turn into brats of the first order. The problem lies in what people here describe as "dysfunctional families." Sometimes it seems as if the whole of America has been counselled into believing that any bad behaviour in an adult is a direct result of problems suffered as a child. In this weird and wonderful society there are groups of militant parents favouring the democratic approach (they're called

STEP, Systematic Training for Effective Parenting) and there are those calling for the return of real discipline (called Back In Control). Some schools in La La Land are so afraid of being sued by angry parents for wrongly disciplining their children, they offer both types of programmes for kids. If that isn't guaranteed to confuse and complicate a child I don't know what is!

The bottom line is that kids here often come packaged in so much cotton wool.

The house we were visiting that day was charming in a rundown sort of way. My friend was leasing it from the family of a well-known film industry figure who had lived in it for nearly thirty years before dying from AIDS a few months previously. Apparently, it came as quite a shock to his two famous daughters to discover that their dearly beloved dad had been leading a secret life as a homosexual for most of their lifetime. Then I heard they were battling with his boyfriend for the majority of the money left in his will.

The problem with this particular house was that the owner had lived happily away from wives and kids for more than thirty years and there were absolutely no safety precautions to prevent the sort of disasters that children can get themselves into.

For starters, the property – which had at one stage been used by Charlie Chaplin to hide the occasional mistress in – had two swimming pools. Then there was a sheer drop of at least fifty feet down to the tennis court, plus the added complication of three tiers of house in that wedding cake design deemed essential if you are constructing a house into the side of a hill.

All four of my kids were old enough to survive each of these potential dangers. However, some of the designer babies on display were not. One particular couple with two toddlers seemed in a state of constant tension when their children attempted to crawl around, as babies tend to.

They were treating their kids as if they were fragile bits of bone china and when the little girl's white designer romper suit got covered in beetroot there was major hysteria. But the thing that most astonished us was that the other daughter appeared to be wearing a pair of her father's Y-fronts around her neck!

The mother explained the reason for this. "She is very close to her father and finds great comfort by hanging them around her neck. She wears them everywhere, including nursery school."

She then revealed she had taken her daughter to a child psychiatrist for analysis.

"But he told me to let her continue doing it for as long as she wanted, just so long as it did not interfere with her socialisation or success in school."

I didn't have the heart to tell her that it might just end up being downright embarrassing for the child when she grew up.

We survived the party without being sued, but I keep wondering how much longer that little girl can walk around with her father's Y-fronts around her neck.

I was casually glancing through the *LA Times* one breakfast time when I stumbled upon the "true" identity of one of my daughter's best friends. La La Land is a very strange place at times.

I examined the photo carefully for at least a couple of minutes before it sunk in that the little girl who had just spent the weekend sleeping over at our house was the alleged lovechild of Robert De Niro. I had to admit I could not see much resemblance between the caucasian actor and the African American child in question, but I had read many times of the Oscar winner's insatiable appetite for duskier women, so it wasn't that much of a surprise.

"BLOOD TESTS ON DE NIRO LOVECHILD CLAIM," screamed the headline. The story underneath revealed that the *Raging Bull* star had been paying child support of around $3,000 a month to the mother since the child's birth ten years earlier, but now she was claiming a much bigger settlement with the help of notorious LA lawyer Marvin Mitchelson, the self-confessed palimony king, whose biggest claim to fame was getting Lee Marvin's live-in love trillions in compensation after they split up.

I wondered what it must be like for this poor child to find herself stuck in the middle of such a highly publicised situation.

She was a quiet child but she clearly loved being with us because we were just an ordinary, noisy, occasionally bad tempered family struggling through life as one compact unit. She loved all the fighting and squabbling that I find so irritating. She loved going to sleep in a bedroom filled with at least three other children. She adored the screaming and shouting in the swimming pool.

A few days later this little girl had to have a blood test in front of a man she had always been told was her father. De Niro had happily paid the monthly sum towards the child's upkeep, but when Mitchleson's palimony team launched a claim for millions, he decided he wasn't certain he was the real father. Ironically, the blood test proved that he was not the biological father and all payments to the mother were stopped.

All thanks to a pushy lawyer and a legal system that long ago went crazy.

Sometime after this, Mitchelson got his 'come-uppence' when he was sentenced to jail for tax evasion. But there is no doubt who the real victims are.

On the last Saturday of the month, I accepted an invitation to go on a deep-sea fishing boat-trip. Visions of *Deliverance* meets *Dead Calm* crossed my mind as I set out at dawn for glitzy Newport Beach and a voyage into the unknown.

This was to be a hail and hearty boys-only trip and my boating comrades included two actors, a movie director, a very astute businessman and little old me. I envisaged being strapped into a soft white Navygatyde fighting chair, pulling in shark after shark before warding the monsters off with vast gaffs on the board at the end of the vessel. This excitement would no doubt be followed by countless gin and tonics back in the harbour that evening.

Newport Beach – about an hour's drive from LA – is filled with pretty little one and two-storey houses and friendly looking bars and restaurants that line the water's edge.

Our boat was a cross between one of those infamous New York tugs and a River Thames houseboat. Fog was drifting across the calm water as the headlights of our car lit up the *Marie Celeste*.

"There she is," our esteemed leader, an American thespian of many years standing, announced with great enthusiasm.

"Ahoy there me hearties," uttered a mountain of a man emerging from below deck with a bottle of something in one hand and a very dead looking bit of bait in the other.

"Welcome aboard. Just getting things prepared here and then we'll be on our way," said Captain Bligh.

The sunrise over the neat wooden rooftops of Newport Beach was glorious. The opulent mansions – with their gardens running down to private quays complete with powerboats – looked like toy dolls' houses backlit by the deep coral rays of light. As the boat chugged slowly towards the harbour entrance and the ocean beyond, we saw real fishermen returning from a long night's work in brightly coloured trawlers filled with yellow tail tuna.

Two tiny objects moved slowly along the middle of the channel in front of us and I realised they were kids – no more than 14-years-old – paddling their surfboards out for an early morning session beyond the harbour wall.

Our first and only port of call before heading for the prime fishing areas about six or seven miles out to sea was a 'baitboat'. These floating pontoons provide thousands of fishermen with their bait and sit bouncing about on the ocean, about one mile out to sea. Our skipper told me an astonishing story about how competition to sell bait in these parts is so fierce that when a newcomer tried to set up a floating bait shop on the same stretch of ocean as a supplier who'd been there for twenty years, his vessel was sunk within days and he was consequently put out of business. Apparently, these sort of 'accidents' frequently occur.

With hundreds of boats passing through each day for $25 worth of bait, I could see that the character who owned that particular business was probably a millionaire quite a few times over. No doubt his wife didn't mind the fact that her husband smelt like Billingsgate on a bad day, just so long as he bought the money home.

Back on the *Marie Celeste*, one of our thespian members of the Famous Five was complaining of feeling weary and we had not even got to our prime fishing location yet. This particular actor is a household name here and in Britain, where he originally comes from. However, the fascinating characters he has played on film and television over the years disguise the fact that he is a rather reserved character. Sadly, in order to survive in the shark infested waters of Hollywood, he had started playing the roles of stereotyped villans in films about such subjects as ninja turtles.

"What time do you think we'll get back tonight?" he asked for the second time, just a few minutes out of Newport Beach.

My fellow Famous Fivers rolled their eyes skywards. This was supposed to be a macho Hemingway-style adventure. We all made a mental note that he was not to be invited on any more Famous Five outings.

The skipper's mate was an odd-looking old chap called

Hubert. He was about five foot tall, with three teeth missing and took regular swigs from a bottle of Jack Daniels. This trip was definitely going to make a change from Disneyland.

Hubert told me he had quit his job as a dental technician in Munich to sail around the world some years earlier.

"I had to leave Germany. It's not like it was in the old days."

I was intrigued. People don't take off like that unless they are running away from something. I probed further and discovered that Hubert had been a U-Boat engineer during the last war and his original plan when setting sail single-handedly was to visit all the ports he had torpedoed between 1942 and 1944.

"I got as far as St. Lucia in the West Indies and then my boat sunk."

That seemed fair enough considering the vast number of ships Hubert had helped sink all those years ago. He never did tell me how he managed to get a ride from St. Lucia to Newport Beach. He took another swig of Jack Daniels before stumbling up the steps that led to the bridge of the *Marie Celeste*. I wondered what state he would be in by the time we actually started fishing.

Two hours later, all of us – with the exception of our homesick, famous face actor – had knocked back a few beers, a wedgeful of sandwiches and were getting nicely scorched by the salt and the sun.

"We'll be there very soon gentlemen," our skipper promised. My earlier fears of a *Deliverance*-style fishing trip had subsided only to be replaced by a distinct feeling that this was turning into more of a *City Slickers* scenario. The skipper was reminding me more and more of Jack Palance.

By midday, none of us had even tried a hand at casting a rod, let alone catching a fish.

Finally, the skipper switched off the throbbing diesels and dropped anchor. The moment to go big-time sport fishing had arrived at last. Five hundred thousand dollar power boats bobbed nearby indicating this was a good catching area. Occasionally, a seagull swooped down to scavenge bits of bait like a rat with wings.

Eventually, we were equipped with bait and rods, but none of us had the ability to actually cast.

"SHIT!"

There was a pained shriek. One of the Famous Five had cast his hook right into the neck of the moaning thespian. We were becoming more like a group of clowns running amok than serious fishermen.

Hubert the mate – now on the second half of his bottle of Jack Daniels – joined forces with one of my pals to try and pull in a monster from the deep. It was putting up one hell of a resistance. Alcohol may have been pickling his brain, but Hubert was determined this one was not going to get away. The two pulled and struggled. Both their faces turned red as they huffed and puffed. "It's a biggun'. I know it is."

The ten inch mackerel looked a little exhausted considering its battle with the two human beings at the other end of the line. Within seconds, it was back in the deep blue ocean heading off for a longer, happier life.

I retreated back into the carpeted galley and listened to Captain Bligh recounting his career as a marine in Vietnam. Soon the rest of the Famous Five were also lurching around with glasses of booze.

On the top deck, our homesick famous face from Britain was still nagging about getting home. His performance was showing Oscar winning potential.

"I was rather hoping I could be back in Malibu in time for supper," he said rather dryly.

"Hard fucking luck," one of my more plain speaking Famous Fivers replied. There was mutiny in the air.

"Why the hell did you come on the boat in the first place?"

Isn't it funny how boat trips bring out the best in people?

166

"HELP! HELP!" yelled our beloved thespian as he struggled to stay afloat off the stern side of the *Marie Celeste*.

"I can't swim. Please help me!"

The mighty skipper threw a life belt into the choppy water. A few moments later, we hauled the precious movie star back on board.

"What happened?"

"He pushed me in. That bastard pushed me in."

He pointed a finger towards his number one enemy, now fast asleep on the deck with Hubert and an empty bottle of Jack Daniels.

Any attempts at fishing soon crumbled and we started mixing glaucomas – a lethal combination of gin, tequila, kahlua, crushed ice, fruit juice, lime and spices – thinking that maybe Hemingway had the right idea when he decided that a .45-calibre submachine gun was the proper tool for deep-sea fishing.

JUNE

It's hard to see where Hollywood ends and the DTs begin.
W. C. Fields

I was casually flicking TV channels one afternoon in June when I came across one of those extraordinary chat shows that seem to dominate TV programming in La La Land. It turned out to be the final piece of inspiration for one of the more important decisions in my life. This programme was doing a feature on young women who marry older men. They had two couples on the programme, a 99-year-old man with his 38-year-old wife, and an 88-year-old man with his 28-year-old wife.

These shows always have a headline as an excuse to get 'interesting' people on their programme. It could be "Women Who Married Transvestites" or "Men Who Pay Their Wives For Sex". I am looking forward to Prince Charles' next visit to the U.S. Then he will no doubt appear on an Oprah Winfrey show entitled "Men Who Drive Their Wives To Bulimia" or maybe Donohue's "Lovers Whose Steamy Phone Calls Are Intercepted".

It was when the 88-year-old husband on this particular show explained that he had a vasectomy thirty years earlier that I turned up the volume. Clare had been requesting that I consider such delicate surgery for quite some time.

A few months earlier, I had discussed it with my wife's gynaecologist – dubbed the housewives' choice by a number of Clare's friends. I had become a trifle niggled by the fact that my wife was forever singing the praises of this handsome heart-throb of a doctor, who spends the majority of his time inspecting parts of the female anatomy only hus-

169

bands and lovers are supposed to reach, and without any of the rules us lesser mortals have to observe.

Going through the 'minor discomfort' of a vasectomy seemed better than Clare's frequent family planning visits to this casanova specialist.

But, along with millions of other men, I feared that a vasectomy could effect impotence and a lot more besides so I had been putting it off. Seeing that elderly man on the screen convincing millions of viewers that a vasectomy had actually improved his love life inspired me to bravely make a momentous decision.

"I've decided to have the snip," I announced to a friend the next day.

He looked baffled.

"A vasectomy. I'm going to have a vasectomy," I said, willing myself to believe it.

He was silent for a while then mumbled:

"We'll do it together."

"What?"

"I said we'll do it together."

Apparently my friend had been thinking about having the operation ever since a macho Italian friend of his had had 'the snip', after getting blind drunk.

"He had to be carried out singing," explained my pal.

"You couldn't get away with that over here." I took a nervous sip of Chardonnay.

"Over here? He had the operation at Cedars-Sinai."

Suddenly, the whole concept of having a vasectomy changed. This could be an excuse to enjoy a day out with a friend, lunch, a few drinks, and then...

"It's $550 for the surgery and $50 for the initial consultation." The female receptionist was stern and humourless.

"Since my friend is coming for the consultation also, I wondered if the doctor would charge $50 for both of us?"

An uncomfortable silence followed. My great pal – who

is a tough-nosed Hollywood producer – had insisted I negotiate with the good doctor. Somehow, he wriggled out of having to deal with it himself.

"I suppose that'll be okay," she said tight-lipped. At least my friend didn't try to make me do a deal with the doctor in which we lay side by side on the gurney and let him 'snip' us both at the same time. A two for the price of one.

"The doctor cannot wait any longer. You'll have to come in and see him without your friend," said the doctor's assistant who reminded me of the evil nurse played so convincingly by Louise Fletcher in *One Flew Over The Cuckoo's Nest*. And I was starting to feel as crazy as Jack Nicholson.

In his office, there was no sign of the man who was about to deprive me of my ability to father children. I noticed that the level of my chair was a foot lower than the good doctor's. Corporate skull-duggery in a doctor's surgery did seem a little power mad for a guy who made his money slicing up men's balls. I panned across the dozens of medical certificates that filled every inch of wall space. Then I looked at the photograph of the doc's glamorous wife and wondered what it must be like to be married to a character who spends much of his day cutting up men's testicles.

No doubt he gets home every evening and she says: "Hello darling had a good day?"

And he replies: "Yes darling, I've sliced up fifteen guys today, so we can afford that ski-ing trip to Aspen this year."

When the good doc finally showed up, he hardly seemed to notice me. A mobile phone was glued to his left ear and another line bleeped on his office phone.

I muttered hello but he still did not acknowledge me, so I just kept quiet. It was like reporting to the headmaster after getting into trouble at school.

"Hi there Mr . . ."

The good doctor was desperately searching for my non-existent file. He clearly did not know my name.

"Mr Clarkson. You're in here for a..."

I was almost ready to forget the whole thing. He did not even realise I was in for a vasectomy. What if he removed my balls by mistake. Anything could happen. *I want outta here!*

"It's a vasectomy. I'm seeing you about a vasectomy." His wrinkly, freckled face peered at me over his spectacles.

"A lot of men get a little scared about the surgery, but it's perfectly safe. You have no need to fear."

He was starting to sound like Dr Crippin.

"But will it affect...?"

"No way will it affect you sex life. The sperms will look just the same. I assure you this surgery will not have any adverse side effects."

He sounded like a tape recorder. The phone rang. It was some poor sod calling from a film shoot in Argentina who was worried because his balls had grown to the size of footballs after allowing the good doc to slice his tubes with a scalpel a week earlier.

"They'll go down. Use lots of ice at night and make sure you don't knock them on anything." *Don't knock them on anything!* How the hell can you avoid it?

The doctor put the phone down and smiled at me.

"Don't worry about a thing. I'll treat them as my own."

I was signing away my life to this guy and now he was cracking jokes.

Ten days later, I was in *Orso's* Restaurant, on Third Street, Beverly Hills, devouring a plate full of the finest linguini as part of our pre-snip celebrations. My friend and I made a toast.

"To the snip. Long may it last."

Just then, we spotted the millionaire doctor who would soon be tampering with our manhood approaching our table.

"The linguini is excellent here. Don't you think?"

He sounded rather like Hannibal Lecter spouting on

about his favourite liver washed down with a fine glass of Chianti. And I don't know if he was joking or not.

He winked at us and walked off, accompanied by an attractive female who was not his wife.

"Have you shaved your balls properly?" my friend asked with a wry smile. The two middle-aged spinsters on the table next to us immediately pricked up their ears.

"What the hell are you talking about?"

"Your balls man. Have you shaved them?"

"You are kidding me?"

"You read those conditions we signed at the consultation last week didn't you?"

It was ten minutes before I underwent surgery and I had not shaved my balls. In La La Land, stores that sell razors tend to be in shopping malls and we were in a stretch of road that consisted soley of Cedar's Sinai Hospital and a few restaurants.

"Waiter. Do you possibly have a razor? I just have to give my chin the quick once over."

I could hear my friend chuckling as I locked myself in the gentlemen's restroom and began slashing away at the offending hairs, at one stage narrowly missing a do-it-yourself vasectomy.

Mission completed, I thanked the waiter profusely. He stared at my still stubbly chin.

"That razor is a bit blunt. I'd throw it away if I were you." I had to tell him something.

A few minutes later, I stumbled nervously into the good doctor's reception area and signed off my cheque for $550. America is the ultimate cash up-front society.

In the tiny operating theatre, I was greeted by a smiling Philippino man and a rather gaunt looking doctor from Moscow, who was over from Russia to learn how to stem their population explosion.

"We'll have to shave you some more Mr Clarkson.

You haven't done a very good job," said the gorilla from Manilla.

I lay there and waited on the slab in a green hospital smock with a strategically placed hole in the middle. The good doc was no doubt untangling himself from someone else's groin before turning up to perform his skills on me.

I felt a hypodermic needle prick into a vein on my arm as he filled my body with Valium. My mind began to wander pleasantly through all sorts of warm and wonderful visions, as down below 'deck', the doc and his gorilla from Manilla began slicing away merrily. I did not bother looking down to see how good their aim was. Instead I gazed up at the ceiling and focused on a rather large spider making its way across one corner.

Suddenly the gorilla from Manilla thrust a glass tumbler under my nose. In it were two tiny pieces of what looked like plastic tubing.

"That's what you English call 'proof of the pudding,'" exclaimed the doctor proudly. He shook the tumbler as if he was about to chuck my tubes on to a nearby table like a pair of dice.

"Wasn't so bad after all. Was it?"

I felt as if I had been kicked in the balls incredibly hard.

Hobbling out into the lobby, I came across my friend look ing a little more anxious than he was earlier. The drink had worn off and the reality of the impending vasectomy was no doubt dawning on him.

"Did it hurt? Did it hurt?"

I tried not to wince as I replied.

"Of course it didn't."

What else could I say?

A few days later – still feeling like a jumbo jet had crash landed on my groin – I foolishly agreed to go to Disneyland with the kids.

As a father of children whose ages range from four to thirteen, I've become an expert on theme parks. There are numerous good ones in La La Land – Disneyland, Six Flags Magic Mountain, Universal Studios and Knottsberry Farm, just to name a few. They are all fairly similar, except for Universal Studios, which actually gives you a sneaky view inside a movie studio.

Six Flags Magic Mountain is advertised as "the thrilling alternative" and it features everything from roaring rapids, a terrifying roller coaster, to a pyrotechnic special – the Batman stunt show. Magic Mountain is about 45 minutes drive north of LA on the Interstate Five freeway.

Knottsberry Farm is better for younger children. You can pan for gold in an Old West Town or ride a steam train. There's even a dinosaur kingdom. To get there head south on Interstate Five and look out for the signs just after the Artesia Freeway.

My personal favourite is Universal Studios. This claims to be the number one movie theme park in the world and attractions include everything from an attack by the star of *Jaws* to experiencing an 8.3 earthquake tremor. Universal is nearer to LA as it sits between Interstates 170 and the 101 just north of Hollywood.

But be warned: Never visit any of these places at weekends if you can avoid it. Mile long queues at every ride can turn the day into a nightmare.

Naturally, we broke this golden rule by going to Disneyland on a scorching hot weekend in June.

We arrived at 9.30 in the morning and by 3.30 that afternoon were totally exhausted and had only been on five proper rides the whole day.

Disneyland is great value for money if you turn up early (around 8.30 even if it doesn't open until 9) and on a weekday. Then move at breakneck speed around the most popular attractions that include my personal recommen-

dations like Star Tours, Captain Nemo's Submarines and
the Big Thunder Mountain Railroad, before the queues
build up (usually by about 11.30am). Then just choose a
couple more rides, have an overpriced, unhealthy lunch and
head back home. I defy anyone with four kids to stay there
the entire day.

On that June afternoon, not only did we fail to get into
most of the rides but I got caught up in a disturbing incident during the scrum for Mickey Mouse's autograph.
Fergus and I were patiently waiting in the queue to speak
with Mickey when a squeaky voice from behind the huge
mouse mask muttered,

"Please. One at a time."

It must have been hot under that costume, even if you
are a Disneyland employee complete with statutory short
hair and straight white teeth.

Just then the surge of little Mickey Mouse fans caused
our hero to lose his footing and collide with one of the
Magic Kingdom street signs. Two pink-stripe shirted Disney
'minders' tried to protect the mouse.

"Please. Some order. Please."

The mouse looked ruffled.

"Assholes," the once-friendly animal hissed.

I pulled Fergus away from the teeming masses and
advised him to try for Snow White's autograph instead.

A few hours later I bundled everyone back into the
Chevy and gratefully hit the freeway back towards LA with
a splitting headache and my balls in agony.

The pain was not much better a few days later when I
went to a breakfast meeting with a celebrated Hollywood
film maker.

The first thing I noticed about *Hugo's Restaurant* on
Santa Monica Boulevard that stuffy June morning was that
nearly all my fellow breakfasters were managing to read

that day's *Variety* while still wearing sunglasses.

Hugo's is the 'in place' to hold important breakfast meetings in tinseltown and I was waiting for the arrival of a very famous director who had shown an interest in one of my screenplays. My hyperactive agent had made the 7.30 am arrangement, convinced that this would impress the movie mogul. She could not have been more wrong.

I'd just settled at a table when a familiar voice wafted over from nearby. I could just make out the features of film star Meryl Streep behind shades asking to borrow the showbiz section of my *LA Times*. I was leaning across with it when a crumpled long-haired man in his mid-fifties shuffled through the door. My breakfast date had arrived. He looked as if he'd been in a bar-room brawl as he collapsed into the seat opposite me.

"You're obviously an early bird," I quipped.

"No fucking way," he replied with a hoarse twang of Joe Cocker in his Geordie voice. "I was told this was the only time you could meet. I hate the fucking mornings."

This meeting was getting off to a good start. We both cursed our agents for ruining any hopes of a lie-in. I was feeling particularly fragile as four-year-old Fergus had spent the entire night waking on the hour.

"I'll take a vegetarian pasta."

It was before 8am but he was ordering lunch. Maybe he was still on London time.

"Best fucking cure for a hangover mate."

And as an afterthought,

"Give me a Becks Beer please."

I settled for cinammon toast and a vodka and orange. If you can't beat 'em . . .

We never did get around to talking about my screenplay. The Top Director had other things on his mind.

"You should have been here in the '70s mate. God they were great. Girls, booze, coke. But now . . . I'm the only person in this town who drinks. It's like a fucking monastery. I hate it."

Here was a guy whose last film had grossed more than a $100 million but he was more interested in talking about wine, women and song.

"Take those fucking condoms. They're fucking useless. I've never been able to make any of them work. Fucking joke if you ask me. I've probably got AIDS, but who gives a shit . . ."

It was around this point that my fourth vodka and orange hit my head like a sledgehammer and sent me off into a pleasant slumber. It wasn't yet 9am and the meeting billed by my agent as the "biggest opportunity you'll ever get in this town" had already collapsed in a heap.

I awoke with a start and for a split second wondered where the hell I was. My ticket to Hollywood stardom had bolted and left me to pay the bill, naturally.

Three weeks later, I phoned his office to request a repeat peformance. One of his assistants rang me back and asked rather curtly: "What exactly is the nature of your inquiry?"

I decided that this was one friendship not worth pursuing.

With my chance at the big time stumbling at the first block, I gratefully took an assignment from a magazine to do a rather predictable piece on the homes of the rich and famous. As a result, I found myself sitting alongside a twitching pilot on a chartered twin-engined Cessna.

The multi-million dollar mansions with their swimming pools and tennis courts looked like scaled down models from 2,500 feet as we swooped over Beverly Hills – the richest piece of real estate in the world. But my mind was on other things, like the pilot's tendency to twitch every 20 seconds.

The photographer sat crouched in the tiny back seat as

I looked dead ahead, frighteningly aware of everything that the pilot could see.

Suddenly, he jerked into a spasm yet again. I was now beginning to suspect he was an epileptic. I just wondered how the hell he got a pilot's licence. This twitch seemed to last an eternity. I looked over my shoulder at the photographer, snapping away at the real estate below, completely oblivious to the health problems of our one and only pilot.

Then the pilot's head jerked back so forcefully I thought it would snap off. Somehow he managed to keep his knee steering the plane on course although we dipped several hundred feet. I didn't need a good imagination to picture the next scene: me struggling to land the aircraft with the pilot slumped in a seizure next to me. Miraculously, he snapped out of his latest attack and regained the plane's rudder. This was turning into more of an adventure than I had envisaged when I accepted the mission earlier that day.

"It's dammed hot, isn't it?" he mumbled, taking off his jacket and flinging open the tiny cockpit window. God knows what was coming next. Earlier I had established – between twitches – that he was a former Thai Airways pilot. He never told me why he left the airline.

His seizures continued for the rest of the flight. The landing was so terrifying I shut my eyes tight and silently prayed as we approached the landing strip at a precarious angle. The twitching pilot was having to steer the plane with his knees at the time. But somehow we made it.

I was so relieved to get on the ground in one piece I didn't say a word when the pilot decided to jump out before the aircraft had stopped moving because he was too hot to wait for the plane to grind to a halt.

Being English in La La Land used to have distinct advantages – until people like Count Guy de Montfort came along.

His real name is Graham Leaver and he hails from the very ordinary town of Dartford, in Kent. But he left a trail of broken-hearted widows after deciding to hit California during my first year in the U.S.

Our two lives collided after I accepted an assignment from a TV programme to produce a documentary on this smooth talking conman, who had been eagerly pursued by the Malibu Sheriff's Department after disappearing with credit cards, cash and jewellery belonging to at least three rather elderly widows from the area.

Leaver fascinated me because he seemed to have the ability to talk himself into any woman's home without giving the slightest hint that he was on the run from prison in Britain and has a criminal record as long as his arm. It has to be said he never physically harmed these women. They were literally swept up by his charming personality. Leaver was like a throw-back to those suave, well spoken confidence tricksters of the fifties.

"He tells a good story. He's quite a charmer. In fact, he's the finest conman I've ever come across," explained Malibu Detective Bill Soltis when I met him to discuss the case.

One of 'Count Con's' first victims on the West Coast was widow Barbara Contratto. She met him in the lobby of the famous Beverly Wilshire Hotel, which Leaver used as his office in the first few weeks after arriving in the States. Within a week he had moved into Barbara's $2 million cliff-top mansion overlooking the Pacific in Malibu and proposed marriage to the quietly-spoken widow. Some time later he disappeared with some of her prized possessions. At least two more vulnerable women followed in fast succession.

Now with this background you would have thought that Leaver would be a difficult chap to track down. All I had was a number for a very shady attorney whom Detective Bill Soltis said had represented Leaver in the past. Graham Leaver was on the phone within minutes of me leaving a message. He said he was desperate to give his side of the story.

We met in a delightful bar in West Hollywood called the *Formosa Cafe*, on Santa Monica Boulevard.

The *Formosa* is a 50-year-old establishment that was once a gathering place for such legendary names as John Wayne and Marilyn Monroe. Its dark and dusky interior bristles with fifties-style furnishings, right down to the red vinyl booth seats.

The *Formosa* is such a Hollywood institution that recent expansion plans by the nearby Warner's Studio had to include $10 million just to move the *Formosa*, brick by brick, to a new location just 250 yards up Santa Monica Boulevard.

I almost got bounced as I waited for Leaver to show up when I completely ignored a quaint old La La Land custom. Apparently, when you pay for a round of drinks with a large bill, the bartender leaves the change on the counter and removes the correct amount from the pile every time you order a subsequent round.

I completely misinterpreted this and accused a particularly large barman of stealing my hard-earned cash after ordering my second vodka martini. But once that little bit of confusion had been cleared up, we got on famously.

Leaver was half an hour late, immaculately dressed and resembled a thinner version of Terry Thomas, even down to the same gap-toothed smile.

"To quote Shakespeare, this is much ado about nothing old chap," said Leaver, whose carefully cultivated English public school accent cleverly hides his more lowly background.

Having persuaded Leaver that TV stardom would undoubtably help him clear his name of "these dreadful accusations", we arranged to film him at a secret address in the San Fernando Valley, where he was hiding out from the women seeking vengeance for the heartbreak he had caused them. He insisted on being called Count Guy de Montfort

181

throughout the interview. There were many classic quotes from Leaver but my favourite was when I asked him if he had promised to marry these lonely women.

"I have not kept a count, but you know what it's like. A chap has to be honorable."

The programme that was eventually aired featured interviews with many of the count's victims, plus a heavy police presence. Leaver did not come out of it well.

Yet less than a week later, I received a reverse charge call from the Terminal Island Prison in Los Angeles. Intrigued by who might be ringing from such a notorious establishment, I accepted the call.

"Hello old chap. I'm in a spot of bother with the Immigration Department and I wondered if you could put up $10,000 bail?"

Graham Leaver – king of the conmen – had not realised that he had been taken himself. Mind you, for a few seconds I did consider helping him.

JULY

*LA is like a big cosy rocking chair; you sit down and by
the time you get up, 40 years have passed.*
Orson Welles

A bus full of German and Japanese tourists stopping to look
at the burnt-out shell of a shopping mall between Vermont
and Normandie was the ultimate proof that life in La La
Land had got back to normal following the riots. As the
beaming visitors pressed their faces against the windows of
the bus, I could hear a soundbite of the tour guide's spiel:

"On your left is some of the most serious damage inflicted
by the worst civil disturbance in U.S. history."

In Britain, there no doubt would be public outrage if
sharp tour operators took advantage of such a tragic situation. But in Los Angeles, this was deemed perfectly
acceptable.

One tour guide assured me there was a "real appetite"
for riot aftermath amongst the hundreds of thousands of
visitors who flock here from around the world each summer.

"I can't take people to downtown L.A. and show them a
few high rises and ignore the wreckage caused by the riots,"
this particular lady told me.

This is a town where a converted Cadillac hearse takes
people to the homes where the rich and famous died in tragic
circumstances. So I suppose a tour of the riot struck areas
doesn't seem so strange.

There are times when I think that surviving in Los Angeles'
film world is all about laughing loudly and talking at the top of
one's voice.

I certainly managed that during a visit to the *Queen Mary*, location of a TV movie backed by a film production company that wanted to buy one of my scripts. The producer had been most insistent that I have lunch with her on the set because she wanted to introduce me to the director and stars in an effort to convince me to sell her my project.

What she did not make clear was that this once renowned floating gin palace had been converted into a rather tacky theme park, complete with reproduction shops, cafes and a constant flow of on board tours at her berth in Long Beach.

The movie, called *Deadly Crossing*, was billed as a "murder on the high seas drama" but when I stumbled onto the set and interrupted an important scene I thought I might become its first real victim.

"CUT!" yelled a first assistant director, glaring at me meaningfully.

I looked suitably apologetic and asked for directions to the production office. As I walked towards the makeshift room constructed out of plywood in the corner of the ship's restaurant, I could hear raised voices.

"I asked for Perrier not Evian!"

One of the stars was having a deep and meaningful discussion with my producer friend. I turned around and waited.

Ten minutes later, the actor emerged grim faced after reluctantly accepting an offer of carbonated mountain spring water.

"Asshole. That's the sort of shit I have to put up with," muttered the producer as I walked in. Producing is a job to be avoided at all costs.

She readjusted her face into charm mode, took me by the arm and waltzed me straight out of her tiny office.

"Let's go see how they are all getting on."

I could have told her the answer without bothering to go back to the set.

"CUT!"

That very noisy assistant director was shouting his favourite word again. This time a party of tourists were strolling through the ballroom.

"The owners refused to stop the tours even though we are filming. Can you believe that?"

I shook my head in wonder. This was not exactly a multi-million dollar production.

Just then an excitable little man with a long nose and huge red glasses rushed up to us.

"Have you seen what those camera tracks have done to my carpet? Have you?"

"Just relax Mr Margolis. We'll take care of it."

"Somebody's dented the wooden panelling in the banqueting suite as well. I should never have let you film here."

Mr Margolis is one of the managers of the *Queen Mary* for whom life on the ocean waves is definitely no bed of roses.

In the corner of the ballroom, actresses Angie Dickinson and Lindsay Wagner cast furtive glances in my direction. But the moment we were introduced and they realised I was not a network executive their interest in me waned.

"The biggest problem is the leading man. He's decided to go back to nature and refuses to use deodorant or brush his teeth," revealed the producer.

It was easy to work out who she was talking about. This particular actor was sitting sullenly in a far corner of the ballroom, all alone.

But my favourite first assistant director was back to being loud again.

"What the hell..."

A star-struck tourist created havoc by wandering onto the set and asking Angie Dickinson for her autograph in the middle of a crucial scene.

"I used to watch you in *Policewoman* when I was a kid," the innocent visitor protested as he was led gently away by a production assistant.

Angie turned to us and shrugged her shoulders.

"I guess I should have stayed in the force..."

A friend in London had told me about the delights of the Hotel Posada de Engelbert. I thought he was kidding as he recounted in vivid detail his four-day adventure at this eccentric watering hole, in La Paz, Mexico. We'd been anxious to explore the Baja – the vast peninsular south of the border – since the first day we decided to move to La La Land.

"Stay at this hotel. You'll love it," promised my pal.

Apparently, the Posada de Engelbert had one very unique aspect. It's owned by middle-aged British crooner Engelbert Humperdinck, the man who once rivalled Tom Jones as the world's most prolific collector of housewives' panties. They still tend to be thrown at him by lusty, thrusting female audiences during sweaty singing sessions at clubs in conservative places like Rapid City, South Dakota.

When I phoned the German manager – and co-owner – of the hotel to make our reservations, he sounded delighted that anyone was booking a room at that time of year.

"You can have any suite you want," said my host. "And you've picked the perfect week because Mr Englebert is here filming with the people from *Lifestyles Of The Rich And Famous*."

The Bavarian born manager – who went by the name of "Hank" – seemed to be completely in awe of his famous partner.

"You should meet Mr Englebert. He's a fascinating character," he promised.

I knew all about heart-throb Humperdinck because the British tabloids for many years used him as fodder for some story or other. The most classic examples that come to mind are "I Had Englebert's Baby, Says Busty Blonde" and "Why

I Love My Wife And Kids, By Engelbert." One tended to follow the other.

Hank happily agreed to a ridiculously cheap room rate so the following week we booked two $200 roundtrip airfares to La Paz, left the kids in the capable hands of our nanny and headed south to the Baja.

La La Landers seem to have some inbuilt fear of Mexico.

"Don't drink the water and take a lot of pills for your stomach," said one lady, whose idea of a vacation was to load her four-wheel drive with every medicine known to mankind and head for a local Holiday Inn.

"Be very careful at night. There are a lot of robberies," warned another Californian, who had never actually been outside his own state, apart from a weekend in Arizona.

Apparently, two-thirds of the viewers who watch the American TV quiz show *Jeopardy* don't even own passports. This country consists of millions of residents who have no wish to venture into the wild and unpredictable outside world, where gas is extremely expensive and drive-in restaurants don't exist.

I ignored all warnings and we set off from LA Airport in a rather cosy, if ancient, Boeing 727 belonging to Mexicana Airways. The old Mexican lady next to me smiled and made the sign of the cross as the jet struggled into the hot, Californian skies.

Two and a half hours later we were making our descent over the sun-baked, white-washed rooftops of La Paz. From the air it looked a lot like the Spain I remembered from my childhood.

I could see tiny horses and carts, and people actually *walking* out on the streets. It seemed a million miles from La La Land. Huge pampas plants lined the airport's only runway, screening dilapidated *casas*, long abandoned to make way for the big metal birds that bring visitors to La Paz.

The sign on the airport terminal said "L-Paz". Somehow that 'a' had disappeared, but I imagine no-one really cared. There were more important things to worry about in life. The gaucho at passport control was just as laid-back. He barely glanced at our passports before he nodded us through.

The ride out to the Posada de Englebert was a bumpy, intimate drive in a mini-bus with eight other tourists. It had grown dark by the time we finally turned down a dusty track. The only light was from the full moon that shone brightly overhead. All eight of us looked nervous when our driver switched off the engine. There were no hotels in sight and the only evidence of life was a handful of white-washed homes.

"Posada de Englebert," uttered the driver. But we seemed to be in the middle of nowhere. He removed our bags from the back and sat them down on the dusty track.

"Aqui?" I uttered in my finest Spanish.

"Si." He pointed to a building shrouded in darkness. A dog barked in the distance.

I peered at the semi-circular sign over the gateway. There had to be some mistake. But the driver was already gratefully accepting my dollars (always preferable to the worthless local pesos). He thrust his finger in the direction of the dark building.

"Si!"

Just then, the sign lit up in a magnificently vulgar display of flickering light bulbs. No seedy neon in La Paz. "Welcome to the Posada de Englebert," it read. I wondered if someone had seen our arrival, or whether Hank had a trip wire near the building which sparked the sign into action whenever anyone got close to the entrance.

Now I could see a vast courtyard, an oval swimming pool and a four sided bar with one lone customer and a very rotund Mexican shaking a cocktail.

We were only a few steps inside the entrance when a

loudspeaker system crackled into action as if it was about to announce a train cancellation on the London Underground. Then I heard it – the unmistakably awful tones of Engelbert's greatest hit, a whining, groaning little number called "Please Release Me". I hoped it wasn't going to sum up our feelings for the Posada de Engelbert.

Clare and I had wanted something different and it seemed we were about to get it. A skinny, beetroot coloured character in his mid-sixties arrived out of nowhere and greeted us like long lost friends.

"Hi. I'm Hank. Welcome to the Posada de Engelbert."

Englebert droned on relentlessly: "Please release me let me go . . ."

Five minutes later, we were settled on a cane bar stool each ordering Margueritas. Jose the bartender offered us a choice: "Americana or a La Paz Marguerita?"

What the hell. We went for the local brew. Jose took down a huge fat bottle shaped like a naked lady and thrust it under our noses. Whatever it was, it was a potent brew.

Two hours later, by which time I could not utter my own name coherently, Hank brought a "very special person" over to the bar to meet us.

When this overweight character in thick horn-rimmed glasses and a miniature pony-tail appeared by my side just after the end of the twelfth rendition of "Please Release Me," I was in no fit state to converse.

"Engelbert. Good to meet you," I managed to mumble.

Clare giggled quietly into her Marguerita, but said nothing.

I didn't dare get off my stool in case I toppled onto the tiled floor. The singing sensation from Leicester stood waiting. Like all good members of the showbiz fraternity he was expecting me to ask the questions.

"Let's have lunch tomorrow," I muttered, hoping I'd be sober by then.

Next morning, we headed for the beautiful stretch of

beach just thirty feet from the front of the hotel. Thickets of flowering plants lined the pathway – Chinese hibiscus, bougainvillaea, sage brush and frangipani.

We clutched the handrail of the precarious steps down to the beach expecting to see rows of sculptured flesh, but there wasn't a thong in sight. No muscled men in Speedos. No bodies working on their tans.

A young boy sat fishing on the end of a broken down jetty with his legs dangling over the edge like Huckleberry Finn. A tatty sign above him read "La Paz Yacht Club".

Yachts bobbed peacefully in the sheltered bay. It was perfect, except that "Please Release Me" was still coming from the beach side bar.

My lunch with Engelbert was a one way flow of conversation involving me asking all the questions and him supplying all the answers.

It must have been 95 degrees as we sat on loungers on the baking sand. Engelbert was wearing his finest dark blue can-you-see-it-no-you-can't G-string. The sweat was pouring off his bronzed, flabby body as fast as he poured the bottle of beer down his throat. I moved into the shade after a few minutes, but he was determined to get a tan before he hit the road for a series of personal appearances beginning in some obscure place in Illinois the following week.

After four ice cold Mexican Sol beers each and a huge plate of nachos Engelbert finally got off the subject of his wonderful career. He pointed to the monastery across the bay.

"See that place over there? Well, I'd like to turn it into a nudist colony."

I tried not to choke on my amber nectar.

"I'm really into clothing optional beaches myself. Went to a great one just north of Santa Barbara recently."

I wondered if I should recommend him to our hotel in Palm Springs. Maybe not . . .

"Really?"

"The monastery would be perfect. Completely isolated. Small one track road. It would be a runaway success."

For some reason, Engelbert reckoned his nudist colony would be a wonderful investment opportunity for a consistently broke writer from La La Land. By the time our lunch ended, Engelbert must have lost a stone in sweat and gained it back in beer consumption.

Clare and I were lying by the pool later when I noticed Hank struggling past with a cooler the size of those heat retainers that doctors transport body parts in, followed by Engelbert and his 27-year-old daughter. They boarded a power boat moored up on the beach in front of the hotel.

"Lucky them," said my wife.

"Lucky us," said I.

Poor old Hank was already as pink as a lobster and I dreaded to think what colour he would be after a few hours out on the wide blue yonder.

As the vessel powered away from the beach, I noticed heart-throb Engelbert struggling up to the front and ever-so-casually removing his G-string before lying out on the deck in all his glory. The old devil was true to his word. He had gone clothing optional.

That evening we escaped from Engelbert and Hank and explored the centre of La Paz. The town has one main road, running alongside the ocean, teeming with people. Mexican cowboys with their girlfriends drifted slowly along in their pick-up trucks, stopping every few yards to chat with friends. Overcrowded buses and sardine can cars crammed with locals were out for a drive in the hot, sticky night. Beautiful dark haired *chicas* wandered up and down the promenade arm in arm with each other, glancing with feigned indifference at the interested men who walked past them. Little children skipped and hopped along the cobbled streets, while their parents looked on from a nearby bar.

The following day we hired a car to explore further afield. Driving in Mexico is no mean feat. Virtually everyone from the local farmer with his horse and cart, to the driver of the biggest truck tends to cut every corner. You frequently find yourself praying before each big bend that nothing is coming in the opposite direction, especially not on your side of the road.

We drove through La Paz's pretty harbour area and soon found ourselves heading north on a marvellous stretch of road looking straight down into the ocean. We passed picturesque communities of white-washed houses and the occasional hotel. Ten foot high cacti dotted the hillside.

Finally, we found what we were looking for – long, completely deserted stretches of sand. No beach bars, no hotels, not even a hint of civilisation. Three vast islands of rock rose out of the ocean like brown icebergs. The smooth surface of the beach indicated that no-one had been here for a long time. Tens of thousands of tiny crabs scurried around making homes for themselves in the sand. Careful not to step on any, we walked down to the water's edge, thankful that there are still some places in the world where the hand of progress has not fallen.

It was time to reflect on our year in La La Land.

We had seen many new places. We had transferred loyalties. We had tried to conquer the language, because a fawcett is really a tap here. We had lapped up the warm and wonderful weather. We had endured floods, earthquakes and riots.

The culture shock of living in La La Land is undeniable. Some days we love it, some days we hate it. But every time I arrive back from a trip away, I feel a definite sense of belonging. It has become our home and I now have a genuine warmth and affection for Los Angeles.

Yet, we had to go through four separate stages in attitude to get to this point.

First there was *The Honeymoon*. For the first few months, each time I drove down Sunset Boulevard, the butterflies in my stomach would flutter with excitement. We had made it! And everything seemed so much larger than life. Everyone was so polite. So caring. So intelligent. Everything was cheaper. Getting adjusted to calling petrol "gas" and asking for the "check" at restaurants seemed so, well, pleasurable. Whenever my children dived into the pool for a swim, I thanked my lucky stars that we were here and not back in drab, grey old Blighty with all its problems.

Then followed *The Bitter and Twisted Phase*. The facade peeled off. La La Land residents started to seem shallow and selfish. Every time a British TV sitcom was shown on TV, we would feel tears welling up. The fact that we never watched these programmes in London was irrelevant. We were missing home. It began to dawn on us that we had left half our lives back home. Everything seemed so much easier in Britain. Suddenly, the language became a problem. Telephone operators became impatient. We began to notice inefficiencies. Little things that previously did not matter suddenly became significant. The rude truck driver we would have ignored a few months earlier now grated. The know-all producer encountered at a dinner party was no longer amusing. But somehow, we got through to the next stage.

The Adjusting. Instead of criticising our U.S. neighbours, we began to recognise the fact that they are no better or worse than people back in Britain. We started to look beneath the surface and ask questions in an effort to understand and appreciate the society more. I even began to adjust to the language. A lift really became an elevator. I stopped asking for rubbers at the stationery store! We had American friends. Things were looking up!

And finally we reached the fourth stage: *Feeling At Home*. Admittedly, it took time. But by the end of a year in La La Land, we could see the locals as individuals and not as a foreign group. And that this was going to be our home for the forseeable future. Interestingly, none of the children seemed to go through these stages to adjust to life in Los Angeles. They simply got on with their lives, making lots of friends and taking full advantage of this weird and wonderful city. We're learning from them...

BIBLIOGRAPHY

NOTE: I have referred to some of these books, newspapers and magazines in the text and they have all provided helpful background information.

Birnbaum's Los Angeles, Harper Collins, New York, 1993.

Raymonde Carroll, *Cultural Misunderstandings*, Harper Collins, New York, 1984.

Judy Cash, *Kidding Around Los Angeles*, John Muir, Sante Fe, N.M., 1989.

Rod Colvin, *Evil Harvest*, Bantam, New York, 1992.

John Gregory Dunne, *The Studio*, Limelight Editions, New York, 1985.

David Freeman, *A Hollywood Education*, Sceptre, New York, 1986.

Frommer's *Los Angeles With Kids*, Prentice Hall, New York, 1993.

William Goldman, *Adventures In The Screen Trade*, Futura, New York, 1985.

E.D. Hirsch, *Cultural Literacy*, Bantam, New York, 1981.

Simon Hoggart, *America – A User's Guide*, Fontana, London, 1991.

LA – My Way, Excellence Enterprises, Sylmar, CA, 1990.

William Meltzer, *L.A. Is The Capital Of Kansas*, Harmony, New York, 1988.

Tom Philbin, *Murder U.S.A.*, Warner, New York, 1992.

Frederick Pratson, *Great Attractions of Los Angeles and Beyond*, Globe Pequot, New York, 1989.

Richard Rayner, *Los Angeles Without A Map*, Paladin, London, 1989.

Gil Reavill, *Los Angeles*, Compass, New York, 1992.

David Reid, *Sex, Death and God in L.A.*, Pantheon, New York, 1992.

David Rieff, *Los Angeles, Capital of the Third World*, Simon and Schuster, New York, 1991.

Esther Wanning, *Culture Shock U.S.A.*, Kuperard, London, 1991.

Alan Whicker, *Whicker's New World*, Coronet, London, 1986.

The Los Angeles Times, 1991 – 1993.
L.A. Style, 1991 – 1993.
Buzz, 1991 – 1993.
Los Angeles Magazine, 1991 – 1993.
Premiere, 1991 – 1993.
Entertainment Weekly, 1991 – 1993.
Movieline, 1991 – 1993.